"Tom Wolfe Has Squeezed a Funny Tale out of Glass and Stone...

a hilarious *opera buffa* starring Mies van der Rohe and Walter Gropius . . . by the time Mr. Wolfe has reached his *coloratura finale,* few have escaped his stiletto."
—*The Wall Street Journal*

". . . a search-and-destroy mission against architectural pretensions . . . the major targets here are those American architects and corporate patrons who betrayed native tastes and traditions . . . a funny book."
—*New York* Magazine

"No wonder . . . this book is the hottest topic in Manhattan's architectural salons . . ."
—*The New York Times Book Review*

"A witty put-down of the architectural frame of mind that turned the American cityscape into a forest of monotonous and often poorly built highrise boxes."
—*Portfolio*

FROM BAUHAUS TO OUR HOUSE
TOM WOLFE

WASHINGTON SQUARE PRESS
PUBLISHED BY POCKET BOOKS
New York   London   Toronto   Sydney   Tokyo

Photo credits: Brent C. Brolin (pp. 9, 57, 68, 69 [top], 87); from *Bauhaus and Bauhaus People* by Eckhard Neumann, copyright © 1970 by Van Nostrand Reinhold Company (p. 13); the Granger Collection (pp. 15, 22, 25, 27, 29, 43); UPI (pp. 37, 74); Don Wallace photo, courtesy of Edgar Tafel (p. 49); Hedrich-Blessing (p. 47); Ezra Stoller © ESTO (pp. 69 [bottom], 82, 106 [middle and bottom]); Edward Durell Stone Associates (pp. 78, 79); © Norman McGrath (p. 106 [top]); Courtesy Max Protetch Gallery (p. 115); © Laurin McCracken (p. 119)

Most of the text originally appeared in the June and July 1981 issues of *Harper's*.

A Washington Square Press Publication of
POCKET BOOKS, a division of Simon & Schuster Inc.
1230 Avenue of the Americas, New York, N.Y. 10020

Published by arrangement with Farrar, Straus & Giroux, Inc.
Library of Congress Catalog Card Number: 81-12589

ISBN: 0-671-68721-2

First Washington Square Press trade paperback printing June 1986

10 9 8 7 6 5 4 3

WASHINGTON SQUARE PRESS and WSP colophon are
registered trademarks of Simon & Schuster Inc.

Printed in the U.S.A.

For Michael McDonough,
who knows where all the acute angles
are hidden in the grid

O BEAUTIFUL, for spacious skies, for amber waves of grain, has there ever been another place on earth where so many people of wealth and power have paid for and put up with so much architecture they detested as within thy blessed borders today?

I doubt it seriously. Every child goes to school in a building that looks like a duplicating-machine replacement-parts wholesale distribution warehouse. Not even the school commissioners, who commissioned it and approved the plans, can figure out how it happened. The main thing is to try to avoid having to explain it to the parents.

Every new $900,000 summer house in the north woods or on the shore of Long Island has so many pipe railings, ramps, hob-tread metal spiral stairways, sheets of industrial plate glass, banks of tungsten-halogen lamps, and white cylindrical shapes, it looks like an insecticide refinery. I once saw the owners of such a place driven to the edge of sensory deprivation by the whiteness & lightness & leanness & cleanness & bareness & spareness of it all. They became desperate for an antidote, such as coziness & color. They tried to bury the obligatory white sofas under Thai-silk throw pillows of every rebellious, iridescent shade of magenta, pink, and tropical green imaginable. But the architect returned, as he always does, like the conscience of a Calvinist, and he lectured them and hectored them and chucked the shimmering little sweet things out.

Every great law firm in New York moves without a sputter of protest into a glass-box office building with concrete slab floors and seven-foot-ten-inch-high concrete slab ceilings and plasterboard walls and pygmy corridors—and then hires a decorator and gives him a budget of hundreds of thousands of dollars to turn these mean cubes and grids into a horizontal fantasy of a Restoration townhouse. I have seen the carpenters and cabinetmakers and search-and-acquire girls hauling in more cornices, covings, pilasters, carved moldings, and recessed domes, more linenfold paneling, more (fireless) fireplaces with festoons of fruit carved in mahogany on the mantels, more chandeliers, sconces, girandoles, chestnut leather sofas, and chiming clocks than Wren, Inigo Jones, the brothers Adam, Lord Burlington, and the Dilettanti, working in concert, could have dreamed of.

Without a peep they move in!—even though the glass box appalls them all.

These are not merely my impressions, I promise you. For detailed evidence one has only to go to the conferences, symposia, and jury panels where the architects gather today to discuss the state of the art. They profess to be appalled themselves. Without a blush they will tell you that modern architecture is exhausted, finished. They themselves joke about *the glass boxes*. They use the term with a snigger. Philip Johnson, who built himself a glass-box house in Connecticut in 1949, utters the phrase with an antiquarian's amusement, the way someone else might talk about an old brass bedstead discovered in the attic.

In any event, the problem is on the way to being solved, we are assured. There are now new approaches, new movements, new isms: Post-Modernism, Late Modernism, Rationalism, participatory architecture, Neo-Corbu, and the Los Angeles Silvers. Which add up to what? To such things as building more glass boxes and covering them with mirrored

Rue de Regret: The Avenue of the Americas in New York. Row after Mies van der row of glass boxes. Worker housing pitched up fifty stories high.

plate glass so as to reflect the glass boxes next door and distort their boring straight lines into curves.

I find the relation of the architect to the client in America today wonderfully eccentric, bordering on the perverse. In the past, those who commissioned and paid for palazzi, cathedrals, opera houses, libraries, universities, museums, ministries, pillared terraces, and winged villas didn't hesitate to turn them into visions of their own glory. Napoleon wanted to turn Paris into Rome under the Caesars, only with louder music and more marble. And it was done. His architects gave him the Arc de Triomphe and the Madeleine. His nephew Napoleon III wanted to turn Paris into Rome with Versailles piled on top, and it was done. His architects gave him the Paris Opéra, an addition to the Louvre, and miles of new boulevards. Palmerston once threw out the results of a design competition for a new British Foreign Office building and told the leading Gothic Revival architect of the day, Gilbert Scott, to do it in the Classical style. And Scott did it, because Palmerston said do it.

In New York, Alice Gwynne Vanderbilt told George Browne Post to design her a French château at Fifth Avenue and Fifty-seventh Street, and he copied the Château de Blois for her down to the chasework on the brass lock rods on the casement windows. Not to be outdone, Alva Vanderbilt hired the most famous American architect of the day, Richard Morris Hunt, to design her a replica of the Petit Trianon as a summer house in Newport, and he did it, with relish. He was quite ready to satisfy that or any other fantasy of the Vanderbilts. "If they want a house with a chimney on the bottom," he said, "I'll give them one." But after 1945 our plutocrats, bureaucrats, board chairmen, CEO's, commissioners, and college presidents undergo an inexplicable change. They become diffident and reticent. All at once they are willing to accept that glass of ice water in the face, that bracing slap across the mouth, that reprimand for the fat on one's bourgeois soul, known as modern architecture.

And why? They can't tell you. They look up at the barefaced buildings they have bought, those great hulking structures they hate so thoroughly, and they can't figure it out themselves. It makes their heads hurt.

1
The Silver Prince

OUR STORY BEGINS in Germany just after the First World War. Young American architects, along with artists, writers, and odd-lot intellectuals, are roaming through Europe. This great boho adventure is called "the Lost Generation." Meaning what? In *The Liberation of American Literature*, V. F. Calverton wrote that American artists and writers had suffered from a "colonial complex" through the eighteenth and nineteenth centuries and had timidly imitated European models—but that after World War I they had finally found the self-confidence and sense of identity to break free of the authority of Europe in the arts. In fact, he couldn't have gotten it more hopelessly turned around.

The motto of the Lost Generation was, in Malcolm Cowley's words, "They do things better in Europe." What was in progress was a postwar discount tour in which practically any American—not just, as in the old days, a Henry James, a John Singer Sargent, or a Richard Morris Hunt—could go abroad and learn how to be a European artist. "The colonial complex" now took hold like a full nelson.

The European artist! What a dazzling figure! André Breton, Louis Aragon, Jean Cocteau, Tristan Tzara, Picasso, Matisse, Arnold Schoenberg, Paul Valéry— such creatures stood out like Gustave Miklos figurines of bronze and gold against the smoking rubble of Europe after the Great War. The rubble, the ruins of European civilization, was an essential part of the picture. The charred bone heap in the background was precisely what made an avant-gardist such as Breton or Picasso stand out so brilliantly.

To the young American architects who made the pilgrimage, the most dazzling figure of all was Walter Gropius, founder of the Bauhaus School. Gropius opened the Bauhaus in Weimar, the German capital, in 1919. It was more than a school; it was a commune, a spiritual movement, a radical approach to art in all its forms, a philosophical center comparable to the Garden of Epicurus. Gropius, the Epicurus of the piece, was thirty-six years old, slender, simply but meticulously groomed, with his thick black hair combed straight back, irresistibly handsome to women, correct and urbane in a classic German manner, a lieutenant of cavalry during the war, decorated for valor, a figure of calm, certitude, and conviction at the center of the maelstrom.

Strictly speaking, he was not an aristocrat, since his father, while well-to-do, was not of the nobility, but people couldn't help thinking of him as one. The painter Paul Klee, who taught at the Bauhaus, called Gropius "the Silver Prince." Silver was perfect. Gold was too gaudy for so fine and precise a man. Gropius

Walter Gropius, the Silver Prince. White God No. 1. Young architects went to study at his feet. Some, like Philip Johnson, didn't get up until decades later.

seemed to be an aristocrat who through a miracle of sensitivity had retained every virtue of the breed and cast off all the snobberies and dead weight of the past.

The young architects and artists who came to the Bauhaus to live and study and learn from the Silver Prince talked about "starting from zero." One heard the phrase all the time: "starting from zero." Gropius gave his backing to any experiment they cared to make, so long as it was in the name of a clean and pure future. Even new religions such as *Mazdaznan*. Even health-food regimens. During one stretch at Weimar the Bauhaus diet consisted entirely of a mush of fresh vegetables. It was so bland and fibrous they had to keep adding garlic in order to create any taste at all. Gropius' wife at the time was Alma Mahler, formerly Mrs. Gustav Mahler, the first and foremost of that marvelous twentieth-century species, the Art Widow. The historians tell us, she remarked years later, that the hallmarks of the Bauhaus style were glass corners, flat roofs, honest materials, and expressed structure. But she, Alma Mahler Gropius Werfel—she had since added the poet Franz Werfel to the skein—could assure you that the most unforgettable characteristic of the Bauhaus style was "garlic on the breath." Nevertheless!—how pure, how clean, how glorious it was to be . . . *starting from zero!*

Marcel Breuer, Ludwig Mies van der Rhoe, Lázló Moholy-Nagy, Herbert Bayer, Henry van de Velde—all were teachers at the Bauhaus at one time or another, along with painters like Klee and Josef Albers. Albers taught the famous Bauhaus *Vorkurs,* or introductory course. Albers would walk into the room and deposit a pile of newspapers on the table and tell the students he would return in one hour. They were to turn the pieces of newspaper into works of art in the interim. When he returned, he would find Gothic castles made of newspaper, yachts made of newspaper, airplanes, busts, birds, train terminals, amazing things. But there would always be some student, a photographer or a glassblower, who would simply have taken a piece of newspaper and folded it once and propped it up like a tent and let it go at that. Albers would pick up the cathedral and the airplane and say: "These were meant to be made of stone or metal—not

The Bauhaus. Gropius' compound itself, built after the Bauhaus moved from Weimar to Dessau in 1925.

newspaper." Then he would pick up the photographer's absentminded tent and say: "But this!—this makes use of the soul of *paper*. Paper can fold without breaking. Paper has tensile strength, and a vast area can be supported by these two fine edges. *This!*—is a work of art in paper." And every cortex in the room would spin out. So simple! So beautiful . . . It was as if light had been let into one's dim brain for the first time. My God!—*starting from zero!*

And why not . . . The country of the young Bauhäusler, Germany, had been crushed in the war and humiliated at Versailles; the economy had collapsed in a delirium of inflation; the Kaiser had departed; the Social Democrats had taken power in the name of socialism; mobs of young men ricocheted through the cities drinking beer and awaiting a Soviet-style revolution from the east, or some terrific brawls at the very least. Rubble, smoking ruins—*starting from zero!* If you were young, it was wonderful stuff. Starting from zero referred to nothing less than re-creating the world.

It is instructive—in view of the astonishing effect it was to have on life in the United States—to recall some of the exhortations of that curious moment in Middle Europe sixty years ago:

"Painters, Architects, Sculptors, you whom the bourgeoisie pays with high rewards for your work— out of vanity, snobbery, and boredom—Hear! To this money there clings the sweat and blood and nervous energy of thousands of poor hounded human beings— Hear! It is an unclean profit . . . we must be true socialists—we must kindle the highest socialist virtue: the brotherhood of man."

So ran a manifesto of the Novembergruppe which included Moholy-Nagy and other designers who would later join Gropius at the Bauhaus. Gropius was chairman of the Novembergruppe's Arbeitsrat für Kunst (Working Council for Art), which sought to bring all the arts together "under the wing of a great architecture," which would be "the business of the entire people." As everyone understood in 1919, *the entire people* was synonymous with *the workers*. "The intellectual bourgeois . . . has proved himself unfit to be the bearer of a German culture," said Gropius. "New, intellectually undeveloped levels of our people are rising from the depths. They are our chief hope."

Gropius' interest in "the proletariat" or "socialism" turned out to be no more than aesthetic and fashionable, somewhat like the interest of President Rafael

Trujillo of the Dominican Republic or Chairman Mao of the People's Republic of China in republicanism. Nevertheless, as Dostoevsky said, ideas have consequences; the Bauhaus style proceeded from certain firm assumptions. First, the new architecture was being created for the workers. The holiest of all goals: perfect worker housing. Second, the new architecture was to reject all things bourgeois. Since just about everyone involved, the architects as well as the Social Democratic bureaucrats, was himself bourgeois in the literal, social sense of the word, "bourgeois" became an epithet that meant whatever you wanted it to mean. It referred to whatever you didn't like in the lives of people above the level of hod carrier. The main thing was not to be caught designing something someone could point to and say of, with a devastating sneer: "How very bourgeois."

Social Democrats in both Germany and Holland were underwriting worker-housing projects and, for their own political reasons, commissioning younger, antibourgeois architects like Gropius, Mies van der Rohe, Bruno Taut, and J. J. P. Oud, who at the age of twenty-eight had been made chief architect of the city of Rotterdam. Oud was a member of a Dutch group known as de Stijl (the Style). The Bauhaus and de Stijl, like the bourgeois-proofed Novembergruppe, were not academies or firms; in fact, they were not like any organizations in the history of architecture prior to 1897. In 1897, in Vienna, a group of artists and architects, including Otto Wagner and Josef Olbrich, formed a group called the Vienna Secession and formally "seceded" from the officially recognized Austrian cultural organization, the Künstlerhaus. Not even the French Impressionists had attempted any such thing; their Salon des Refusés had been but a noisy cry to the National Institute: We want *in!* The Vienna Secession (and those in Munich and Berlin) originated an entirely novel form of association, the art compound.

In an art compound you announced, in one way or another, usually through a manifesto: "We have just removed the divinity of art and architecture from the hands of the official art establishment [the Academy, the National Institute, the Künstlergenossenschaft, whatever], and it now resides with us, inside our compound. We no longer depend on the patronage of the nobility, the merchant class, the state, or any other outside parties for our divine eminence. Henceforth, anyone who wishes to bathe in art's divine glow must come here, inside our compound, and accept the forms we have created. No alterations, special orders, or loud talk from the client permitted. We know best. We have exclusive possession of the true vision of the future of architecture." The members of a compound formed an artistic community, met regularly, agreed on certain aesthetic and moral principles, and broadcast them to the world. The Vienna Secession—like the Bauhaus twenty-five years later—built an actual, physical compound in the form of an exemplary building, the House of Secession, which they called "a temple of art."

The creation of this new type of community proved absolutely exhilarating to artists and composers, as well as architects, throughout Europe in the early years of this century. We're independent of the bourgeois society around us! (They became enamored of this term *bourgeois.*) And superior to it! It was the compounds that produced the sort of avant-gardism that makes up so much of the history of twentieth-century art. The compounds—whether the Cubists,

Fauvists, Futurists, or Secessionists—had a natural tendency to be esoteric, to generate theories and forms that would baffle the bourgeoisie. The most perfect device, they soon discovered, was painting, composing, designing *in code*. The peculiar genius of the early Cubists, such as Braque and Picasso, was not in creating "new ways of seeing" but in creating visual codes for the esoteric theories of their compound. For example, the Cubist technique of painting a face in cartoon profile, with both eyes on the same side of the nose, illustrated two theories: (1) the theory of flatness, derived from Braque's notion that a painting was nothing more than a certain arrangement of colors and forms on a flat surface; and (2) the theory of simultaneity, derived from discoveries in the new field of stereoptics indicating that a person sees an object from two angles simultaneously. In music, Arnold Schoenberg began experiments in mathematically coded music that proved baffling to most other composers, let alone the bourgeoisie—and were all the more irresistible for it, in the new age of art compound.

Composers, artists, or architects in a compound began to have the instincts of the medieval clergy, much of whose activity was devoted exclusively to separating itself from the mob. For mob, substitute bourgeoisie—and here you have the spirit of avant-gardism in the twentieth century. Once inside a compound, an artist became part of a clerisy, to use an old term for an intelligentsia with clerical presumptions.

But what was supposed to be the source of a compound's authority? Why, the same as that of all new religious movements: direct access to the godhead, which in this case was Creativity. Hence, a new form of document: the art manifesto. There were no manifestos in the world of art prior to the twentieth century

and the development of the compounds. The Italian
Futurists delivered the first manifesto in 1910. After
that, there was no stopping the various movements
and isms. They began delivering manifestos day and
night. A manifesto was nothing less than a compound's Ten Commandments: "We have been to the
top of the mountain and have brought back the Word,
and *we now declare that—*"

Of course, it was one thing for artists—the Futurists, Vorticists, Orphists, Purists, Dadaists, Surrealists—to come down from the mountaintop with their
commandments and declarations of independence and
promethean aloofness to the bourgeoisie. It was quite
another for architects, dependent, as they were, upon
the favor of the usually conservative—and, if one need
edit, bourgeois—elements who had the money needed
to erect buildings. Amazingly enough, however, the
strategy worked the very first time it was tried, by the
Vienna Secession itself. Thanks to an accident of Austrian history, the government actually stepped in (inside the compound) and honored the Secession's outrageous claims. There was a period of about five years
when Otto Wagner and the others received important
commissions.* That was all it took. The notion of the
uncompromisable architect became highly contagious.
Before the First World War, the privately financed
Deutsche Werkbund had set about designing the perfect forms of architecture and applied arts for all of
Germany. (The client, naturally, was supposed to
clamor to come inside and get some.) Gropius had
been one of the Werkbund's leading figures.

---

*The government thought (quite mistakenly) that a new and cos-
mopolitan architecture might help transcend the country's bitter ra-
cial and ethnic hostilities.

After the war, various compounds—Bauhaus, Wendingen, de Stijl, Constructivists, Neoplasticists, Elementarists, Futurists—began to compete with one another to establish who had the purest vision. And what determined purity? Why, the business of what was bourgeois (sordid) and what was nonbourgeois (pure).

The battle to be the least bourgeois of all became somewhat loony. For example, early in the game, in 1919, Gropius had been in favor of bringing simple craftsmen into the Bauhaus, yeomen, honest toilers, people with knit brows and broad fingernails who would make things by hand for architectural interiors, simple wooden furniture, simple pots and glassware, simple this and simple that. This seemed very working class, very nonbourgeois. He was also interested in the curvilinear designs of Expressionist architects such as Erich Mendelsohn. Mendelsohn's dramatic curved shapes exploded all bourgeois conceptions of order, balance, symmetry, and rigid masonry construction. Yes—but a bit naïve of you all the same, Walter! In 1922 the First International Congress of Progressive Art was held in Düsseldorf. This was the first meeting of compound architects from all over Europe. Right away they got down on the mat over this business of *nonbourgeois*. Theo van Doesburg, the fiercest of the Dutch manifesto writers, took one look at Gropius' Honest Toilers and Expressionist curves and sneered and said: *How very bourgeois.* Only the rich could afford handmade objects, as the experience of the Arts and Crafts movement in England had demonstrated. To be nonbourgeois, art must be machine-made. As for Expressionism, its curvilinear shapes defied the machine, not the bourgeoisie. They were not only expensive to fabri-

Erich Mendelsohn's Einstein Tower observatory, the ulti-mate example of Expressionist architecture.

cate, they were "voluptuous" and "luxurious." Van Doesburg, with his monocle and his long nose and his amazing sneer, could make such qualities sound bourgeois to the point of queasiness. Gropius was a sincerely spiritual force, but he was also quick enough and competitive enough to see that van Doesburg was backing him into a dreadful corner.

Overnight, Gropius dreamed up a new motto, a new heraldic device for the Bauhaus compound: "Art and Technology—a New Unity!" Complete with exclamation point! *There;* that ought to hold van Doesburg and the whole Dutch klatsch. Honest toilers, broad fingernails, and curves disappeared from the Bauhaus forever.

But that was only the start. The definitions and claims and accusations and counteraccusations and counterclaims and counterdefinitions of what was or was not bourgeois became so refined, so rarefied, so arcane, so dialectical, so scholastic . . . that finally building design itself was directed at only one thing: illustrating this month's Theory of the Century concerning what was ultimately, infinitely, and absolutely nonbourgeois. The buildings became theories constructed in the form of concrete, steel, wood, glass, and stucco. (Honest materials, nonbourgeois, theory of.) Inside and out, they were white or beige with the occasional contrasting detail in black or gray. Bruno Taut, who was a member of Mies van der Rohe's new group, the Ring, had designed his part of the Hufeisen worker housing project in Berlin with red façades. "Red front!" he would yell, just in case there was someone too dense to get the point. Bruno was a likable sort. And God knew he was profoundly nonbourgeois . . . on the emotional and intellectual level . . . After all, he was a Marxist to the point of popped veins on the forehead. He was the kind of man they had naturally assigned to do a worker housing project called Uncle Tom's Cabin *(Onkel Toms Hütte)* in Berlin. But a red façade? A *color?* Well, I mean, my God—*how very bourgeois!* Why didn't he go all the way and put nasturtiums all over the front, the way Otto Wagner did with his Majolika House in Vienna in 1910! Oh, how they sniggered at poor Bruno over his beloved red front. Henceforth, white, beige, gray, and black became the patriotic colors, the geometric flag, of all the compound architects.

So goodbye, color. On spun that holy tornado, Theory, until buildings by compound artists were aimed at very little else. They became supremely, divinely nonfunctional, even though everything was done in the name of "functionalism," functional being one of several euphemisms for nonbourgeois.

For example, there was the now inviolable theory of the flat roof and the sheer façade. It had been decided, in the battle of the theories, that pitched roofs and cornices represented the "crowns" of the old nobility, which the bourgeoisie spent most of its time imitating. Therefore, henceforth, there would be only flat roofs; flat roofs making clean right angles with the building façades. No cornices. No overhanging eaves. These young architects were working and building in cities like Berlin, Weimar, Rotterdam, Amsterdam, at about the Fifty-second Parallel, which also runs through Canada, the Aleutian Islands, Moscow, and Siberia. At this swath of the globe, with enough snow and rain to stop an army, as history had shown more than once, there was no such thing as a functional flat roof and a functional façade with no overhang.* In fact, it is difficult to imagine where such a building might be

---

*It was sometimes permissible to construct a "mono-pitch" roof, a roof with one sloping surface instead of two; and this exception to the rule for worker housing in the 1920s is given devout homage today, on a gigantic scale, in such office towers as the Citicorp Building in New York and Pennzoil Place in Houston.

considered functional, outside of the Painted Desert. Nevertheless, there was no turning back from the flat roof and the sheer façade. It had become the very symbol of nonbourgeois architecture. No eaves; so that very quickly one of the hallmarks of compound work, never referred to in the manifestos, became the permanently streaked and stained white or beige stucco exterior wall.

Then there was the principle of "expressed structure." The bourgeoisie had always been great ones for false fronts (it hardly needed saying), thick walls of masonry and other grand materials, overlaid with every manner of quoin and groin and pediment and lintel and rock-faced arch, cozy anthropomorphic elements such as entablatures and capitals, pilasters and columns, plinths and rusticated bases, to create the

Le Corbusier's Villa Savoye. Flat roof. Sheer façade. White stucco. And "pilings" (pilotis). "Columns" was a bourgeois word.

impression of head, midsection, and foot; and every manner of grandiose and pointless gesture—spires, Spanish tile roofs, bays, corbels—to create a dishonest picture of what went on inside, architecturally and socially. All this had to go. All masonry, all that gross and "luxurious" granite, marble, limestone, and red brick was suspect, unless used in obviously non-load-bearing ways. Henceforth walls would be thin skins of glass or stucco. (Small glazed beige ceramic bricks were okay in a pinch.) Since walls were no longer used to support a building—steel and concrete or wooden skeletons now did that—it was dishonest to make walls look as chunky as a castle's. The inner structure, the machine-made parts, the mechanical rectangles, the modern *soul* of the building must be expressed on the outside of the building, completely free of applied decoration. The ultimate expression of this principle was the de Stijl architect Gerrit Rietveld's Schroeder House. Rietveld covered the exterior in projections whose only function was to indicate the grid, the diagram, the paradigm, the geometric progression on which the plans were based. Astonishing! What virtuosity! How very nonbourgeois.

So, in the world of the architectural compounds, competition now took place on two levels. There was not merely the age-old competition to obtain commissions and get the chance to show the world what you could do by designing buildings and seeing them go up. There was also the sheerly intellectual competition of the theories. Since the divinity of art now resided inside the compounds and nowhere else, there was nothing to keep a man of inspiration and genius, a priest, a hierophant, a Duns Scotus, from making a name for himself without even leaving the priestly walls. Thus

*Gerrit Rietveld's Schroeder House. The Dutch really knew
how to bourgeois-proof a building.*

there came into being another unique phenomenon:
the famous architect who did little or no building.

The first of these had been the Futurist Sant'Elia,
with his visionary buildings for the Milan of the future,
which he rendered in great detail in the years before
the war. But Sant'Elia, who died in the war, was nothing compared to the Swiss-born star of the Paris art
world, Le Corbusier. Le Corbusier was the sort of
relentlessly rational intellectual that only France loves
wholeheartedly, the logician who flies higher and
higher in ever-decreasing concentric circles until, with
one last, utterly inevitable induction, he disappears up
his own fundamental aperture and emerges in the
fourth dimension as a needle-thin umber bird.

Le Corbusier's instincts for the compound era were
flawless. Early on, he seemed to comprehend what

became an axiom of artistic competition in the twentieth century. Namely, that the ambitious young artist *must* join a "movement," a "school," an ism—which is to say, a compound. He is either willing to join a clerisy and subscribe to its codes and theories or he gives up all hope of prestige. One rummages in vain through the history of art and architecture since 1900 for the figure of great prestige who, in the Thoreau manner, marches to a different drummer, the solitary genius whose work can only be described as *sui generis*. (With the possible exception of Frank Lloyd Wright, whose fate we will observe in a moment.) No, the much-acclaimed solitary figure one finds instead is the artist or architect who, like Kasimir Malevich, is smart enough to cover himself in the trappings of a movement, an ism, and becomes a one-man compound. Or, if he can find a pal, a two-man compound. Whereupon he shouts: "I am a Suprematist! [or a Purist! or an Orphist!] Don't think I'm out here by myself! The rest of my boys will be here any minute!" Le Corbusier hooked up with his pal Amédée Ozenfant—and became Purism.

Le Corbusier was a thin, sallow, nearsighted man who went about on a white bicycle, wearing a close-fitting black suit, a white shirt, a black tie, round black owl-eye glasses, and a black bowler hat. To startled onlookers, he said he dressed in this fashion so as to look as neat and precise and anonymous as possible, to be the perfect mass-producible wire figure for the Machine Age. He called the houses he designed "machines for living." Le Corbusier traveled to Germany and Holland and was well known in all the compounds and at all the congresses, conferences, symposia, and panel discussions, wherever the insistent beat of the manifesto, the song of the compounds was heard: *We*

Le Corbusier. Mr. Purism. He showed everybody how to become a famous architect without building buildings. He built a Radiant City inside his skull.

declare—! We declare—! We declare—! We declare—! He was intense, he was riveting, he was brilliant, he was Aquinas, the Jesuits, Doctor Subtilis and the Scholastics, Marx, Hegel, Engels, and Prince Kropotkin all rolled into one. His *Vers une architecture* was a scripture. By 1924 he was one of the reigning geniuses of the new architecture. In his world he was . . . *Corbu!* the way Greta Garbo was *Garbo!* in hers; all on the strength of his manifesto, his zealotry, and a handful of little houses: for his brother, for Ozenfant, for kinfolk and bohofolk. Next came one for Mom and Dad. The retirement house for Mother, which she paid for and put up with, became the very insignia of the compound architect.

It was Le Corbusier's particularly sad fate to live and work in France. Who in France was going to meet the terms of an architectural compound? Which were: "Henceforth, anyone who wishes to bathe in that divine glow must come here, inside the compound, and accept the forms we have created. No alterations or special orders and no loud talk from the client permitted." Who, indeed! Practically no one, unless possessed with a Corbu mother's love or fascinated with Le Moderne, such as the developer Frugés, who commissioned Le Corbusier to do some low-rent apartments in the Bordeaux town of Pessac in 1925. Most mortals who were in a position to commission buildings wanted the Beaux-Arts style, the latter-day synthesis of the Classical revivals that had begun in the Renaissance. The compounds had no *public,* no *clientele,* in the ordinary sense. The brutal fact of life was that it was difficult for compound architects to get work unless there was a government—usually socialist—that had decided, in effect: We need a new look around here, and you fellows have one. Here's the budget; go to it; do what you will.

As it turned out, it was the German Social Democratic government in Stuttgart that gave Le Corbusier one of the first major commissions of his career. This was in 1927, and he had Mies van der Rohe to thank.

The Stuttgart government put Mies in charge of a worker-housing exhibition, the Weissenhof Werkbund project. Despite an extremely tight budget, Mies managed to turn the project into a world's fair of worker housing. He brought in Le Corbusier from France, Oud and Mart Stam from Holland, and Victor Bourgeois from Belgium to join him and eleven other Germans, including Gropius, Bruno Taut, Bruno's brother Max, and Peter Behrens. Outsiders were amazed at the harmony or sameness (according to whether they liked the style or didn't) of the work of these architects from four different countries. It was as if a new *international style* were in the wind. The truth was that the internal mechanism of the compound competition, the everlasting reductionism—*nonbourgeois!*—had forced them all within the same tiny cubicle, which kept shrinking, like the room in Poe's "The Pit and the Pendulum." Short of giving up the divine game altogether, they couldn't possibly have differed from one another in any way visible to another living soul on this earth save another compound architect outfitted, like a cryptographer, with Theory glasses.

And how did worker housing look? It looked nonbourgeois within an inch of its life: the flat roofs, with no cornices, sheer walls, with no window architraves or raised lintels, no capitals or pediments, no colors, just the compound shades, white, beige, gray, and black. The interiors had no crowns or coronets, either. They had pure white rooms, stripped, purged, liberated, freed of all casings, cornices, covings, crown moldings (to say the least), pilasters, and even the ogee edges on tabletops and the beading on drawers. They had open floor plans, ending the old individualistic, bourgeois obsession with privacy. There was no wallpaper, no "drapes," no Wilton rugs with flowers on them, no lamps with fringed shades and bases that look like vases or Greek columns, no doilies, knickknacks, mantelpieces, headboards, or radiator covers. Radiator coils were left bare as honest, abstract, sculptural objects. And no upholstered furniture with "pretty" fabrics. Furniture was made of Honest Materials in natural tones: leather, tubular steel, bentwood, cane, canvas; the lighter—and harder—the better. And no more "luxurious" rugs and carpets. Gray or black linoleum was the ticket.

And how did the workers like worker housing? Oh, they complained, which was their nature at this stage of history. At Pessac the poor creatures were frantically turning Corbu's cool cubes inside out trying to make them cozy and colorful. But it was understandable. As Corbu himself said, they had to be "reeducated" to comprehend the beauty of "the Radiant City" of the future. In matters of taste, the architects acted as the workers' cultural benefactors. There was no use consulting them directly, since, as Gropius had pointed out, they were as yet "intellectually undeveloped." In fact, here was the great appeal of socialism to architects in the 1920s. Socialism was the political answer, the great yea-saying, to the seemingly outrageous and impossible claims of the compound architect, who insisted that the client keep his mouth shut. Under socialism, the client was the worker. Alas, the poor devil was only just now rising up out of the ooze. In the meantime, the architect, the artist, and the intellectual would arrange his life for him. To use Stalin's phrase, they would be the engineers of his soul. In his apartment blocks in Berlin for employees of the Siemens factory, the soul engineer Gropius decided that the workers should be spared

high ceilings and wide hallways, too, along with all of
the various outmoded objects and decorations. High
ceilings and wide hallways and "spaciousness" in all
forms were merely more bourgeois grandiosity, expressed in voids rather than solids. Seven-foot ceilings
and thirty-six-inch-wide hallways were about right for
. . . re-creating the world.

Starting from zero! Well, my God! The American pilgrims, the young American architects who were making the discount tour of Europe—Louis Kahn, Edward
Durell Stone, Louis Skidmore, and many others—had
only to compare the position of these young men to
their own. What was the best a young architect could
hope for in America? If he were extremely fortunate,
he might be commissioned to design a weekend home
on the North Shore of Long Island for some Wall
Street hardgrabber. Louis Kahn's friend George Howe
liked to say: "We used to give them Norman country
manors with everything but the pile of manure in the
yard." Terrific. The height of excitement in American
architectural circles was those brave new styles,
North Shore Norman and Westchester Tudor, also
known as Half-timber Stockbroker. What a goal to
aspire to . . . as compared to . . . *re-creating the world!*
    Heretofore the American architect had been a man
whose job was to lend coherence and detail to the got-
rocks romantic fantasies of capitalists. But now, in
Europe, you saw groups of architects working with the
godly autonomy of the greatest artists.
    No, the approach of the European compounds, of
Gropius and the Bauhaus, of Mies, Corbu and de Stijl,
was utterly irresistible. There were several problems
to be overcome, however. To begin with, the notion of
starting from zero made no sense at all in the United

States. The sad truth was that the United States had not been reduced to a smoking rubble by the First World War. She had emerged from the war on top of the world. She was the only one of the combatants who had not been demolished, decimated, exhausted, or catapulted into revolution. She was now one of the Great Powers, young, on the rise, bursting with vigor and rude animal health. Not only that, she had no monarchy or nobility to be toppled, discredited, blamed, vilified, or otherwise reacted against. She didn't even have a bourgeoisie. In the absence of a nobility or any tradition of one, the European concept of the bourgeoisie didn't apply. (American writers, dazzled by the European stance, imported it anyway, like a pair of Lobb shoes or a jar of Beluga caviar, and began talking about "the booboisie," "Babbitt," "boosterism," and the rest of it.) There was very little interest in socialism. There was not even any interest in worker housing. Nobody even talked about it.

Nevertheless . . . it had to be! How could anyone turn back after having seen the Radiant City? The great new European architectural vision of Worker Housing would have to be brought to America by any means necessary, in any form necessary. *Any* form.

O young silver princes set against the rubble!

2

Utopia Limited

SO IT WAS that one of the most dotty and influential documents in the entire history of the colonial complex came to be written. This was a piece called "The International Style," by Henry-Russell Hitchcock and Philip Johnson, the twenty-six-year-old son of a wealthy Cleveland lawyer. The boy had given the Museum of Modern Art the money to found an architecture division, which he then headed. Hitchcock and Johnson wrote "The International Style" for the catalogue of the museum's 1932 show of photographs and models aimed at introducing the work of Gropius et alii to New York. The term "International Style" was taken from the title of a book Gropius had published seven years before, *International Architecture*.

Museum catalogue copy, which is a species of forced labor or gun-at-the-temple scholarship, is notorious for its sophistry, when it isn't patent nonsense. But "The International Style" was literature of a higher order. It *shone* . . . with the hallucinatory clarity of a Church of the Galilee Walker handbill. The two men were baying at a silvery, princely moon.

In utter seriousness they set up a distinction between *architecture* and *building,* after the manner of Vitruvius some two thousand years before. The italics, presumably, were meant to indicate that these were objective, scientific categories. In Europe, Gropius, Mies van der Rohe, Le Corbusier, and Oud—the four great "European functionalists," as Hitchcock and Johnson called them—were creating *architecture.* In America, even the architects who thought they were being modern and functional were only engaged in *building.* Oh, there was always Frank Lloyd Wright, of course . . . and with a certain weariness Hitchcock and Johnson paid him homage for his work . . . in the distant past . . . and then concluded that he was merely "half-modern." Which was to say, he was finished and could be forgotten.

As for the pride of twentieth-century American architecture, the skyscraper, it was all they could do to contain their amusement. The skyscrapers were empty compositions tarted up with "zigzag trimmings" and God knew what else. American architects, and skyscraper architects most especially, were always willing to "deface" their buildings with bad design, if the client demanded it. The Europeans, they implied, would walk away from a commission before submitting to any such stupidity.

In his preface to the book version of *The International Style,* the Museum of Modern Art's director, Alfred Barr, took a look at the finials, the *crowns,* of New York's most famous skyscrapers. He was appalled. "The stainless-steel gargoyles of the Chrysler Building," "the fantastic mooring mast atop the Empire State"—how could such vulgarities come into being? Simple: American architects stood still and listened to the client. He had even heard architects

The Empire State Building (left) and the Chrysler Building.
Oh, how they sniggered at the little Christmas-tree orna-
ments on top!

argue, albeit cynically, that their hideous little orna-
ments and hollow grandiosities were "functional,"
since one function of a building was to please the
client. "We are asked," said Barr, "to take seriously
the architectural taste of real-estate speculators, rent-
ing agents, and mortgage brokers!"

Hitchcock and Johnson spent many pages analyzing
the designs of the great "functionalists"—and none
analyzing such inconvenient matters as the workers,
worker housing, and socialism, much less the slightly
mad battles of the compounds. There was only the
occasional cryptic remark about how American architects could not "claim for their skyscrapers and

apartment houses the broad sociological justification that exists for the workers' housing, the schools and hospitals of Europe."

In fact, they gave no indication that the International Style—and their label caught on immediately—had originated in any social setting, any terra firma, whatsoever. They presented it as an inexorable trend, meteorological in nature, like a change in the weather or a tidal wave. The International Style was nothing less than the first great universal style since the Medieval and Classical revivals, and the first truly modern style since the Renaissance. And if American architects wanted to ride the wave, rather than be wiped out by it, they had first to comprehend one thing: the client no longer counted for anything except the funding. If he were cooperative, not too much of a boor, it was acceptable to let him benefit from your new vision. How this was to work out in practice, they didn't say. How much explaining did a tidal wave have to do?

The show and the catalogue created a terrific stir in the American architectural community, chiefly because of the status of the museum itself. The Museum of Modern Art was the colonial complex inflated to prodigious dimensions. In Europe, avant-garde movements, whether the Fauvists, the Cubists, the Neoplasticists, or the Bauhaus, were initiated and developed by artists and architects. In Europe, that went without saying. At a later stage, as in Vienna after the turn of the century and in Paris and London in the early 1920s, the more adventurous businessmen and other members of the bourgeoisie might give them their support, for reasons of politics or cultural piety or simply to appear chic, "modern," and not bourgeois at all. Only in America did it happen exactly the other way around. Only in America did businessmen and their wives introduce avant-garde art and architecture and carry the brave banner forward and urge the practitioners to follow, if they could possibly find the wit to catch on.

The Museum of Modern Art, after all, was not exactly the brainchild of socialists or visionary bohemians. It was founded in John D. Rockefeller, Jr.'s living room, to be exact, with A. Conger Goodyear, Mrs. Cornelius Newton Bliss, and Mrs. Cornelius J. Sullivan in attendance. They had seen their counterparts in London enjoying the chic and excitement of Picasso, Matisse, Dérain, and the rest of Le Moderne and were determined to import it to New York for themselves. In 1929 the museum opened, and European modernism in painting and sculpture was established, *institutionalized,* overnight, in the most overwhelming way, as the new standard for the arts in America. The International Style exhibition was designed to do the same thing for European modernism in architecture.

Our visionary avant-gardists! Rockefellers, Goodyears, Sullivans, and Blisses! O oil men, lumber men, dry-goods jobbers, and wives!

It was marvelous. It was like the plot of Gilbert and Sullivan's opera *Utopia Limited.* King Paramount, ruler of a tropical paradise, having heard that the English were the last word in all matters of dress, speech, manners, and cultivation, converts his court to the English style. He and his retainers step straight out of their muumuus, palm fronds, and orchid blossoms into britches, frock coats, wigs, corsets, hollyhock skirts, and pointed shoes. He orders his subjects to follow suit. Baffled but impressed, they do so.

In the opera, as one might well predict, the king and

his countrymen discover, by and by, that the native ways were best after all; and the last laugh is on the Europeans. There Gilbert and Sullivan and the New York art world part company. Not for a moment did the oil men and the lumber men or their subjects—the artists—have the slightest doubt that the European way was best. Throughout the 1930s, the local artists, notably Arshile Gorky, groused and grumbled and protested that the museum devoted all its resources to European work and never gave them a chance. But they didn't have their hearts in it. The colonial complex had become so intense that the standard response to the reputation of the Europeans was not to compete with them but to imitate them, often with total frankness.

Gorky's model was Picasso, and he didn't care who knew it. A friend told Gorky that, in his opinion, Picasso's recent work was lazy and sloppy. In many canvases his edges were blurred. There were even drips of paint.

"If Picasso blurs," said Gorky, "then I blur. If he drips, I drip."

In the next moment, however, his whole stance would seem hopeless. He would fall into depressions. One day he called a meeting of all the artists he knew in his studio.

"Let's face it," he told them. "We're bankrupt."

Such was the mental atmosphere into which Hitchcock and Johnson introduced the International Style. Little did they know that they were but the messenger Elijahs, the Mahaviras, the Baptist heralds for an event more miraculous than any they would have dared pray for: the coming.

3

The White Gods

ALL AT ONCE, in 1937, the Silver Prince himself was here, in America. Walter Gropius; in person; in the flesh; and here to stay. In the wake of the Nazis' rise to power, Gropius had fled Germany, going first to England and coming now to the United States. Other stars of the fabled Bauhaus arrived at about the same time: Breuer, Albers, Moholy-Nagy, Bayer, and Mies van der Rohe, who had become head of the Bauhaus in 1930, two years after Gropius, already under pressure because of the left-wing aura of the compound, had resigned. Here they came, uprooted, exhausted, penniless, men without a country, battered by fate.

Gropius had the healthy self-esteem of any ambitious man, but he was a gentleman above all else, a gentleman of the old school, a man who was always concerned about a sense of proportion, in life as well as in design. As a refugee from a blighted land, he would have been content with a friendly welcome, a place to lay his head, two or three meals a day until he could get on his own feet, a smile every once in a while, and a chance to work, if anybody needed him. And instead—

The reception of Gropius and his confreres was like a certain stock scene from the jungle movies of that period. Bruce Cabot and Myrna Loy make a crash landing in the jungle and crawl out of the wreckage in their Abercrombie & Fitch white safari blouses and tan gabardine jodhpurs and stagger into a clearing. They are surrounded by savages with bones through their noses—who immediately bow down and prostrate themselves and commence a strange moaning chant.

The White Gods!
Come from the skies at last!

Gropius was made head of the school of architecture at Harvard, and Breuer joined him there. Moholy-Nagy opened the New Bauhaus, which evolved into the Chicago Institute of Design. Albers opened a rural Bauhaus in the hills of North Carolina, at Black Mountain College. Mies was installed as dean of architecture at the Armour Institute in Chicago. And not just dean; master builder also. He was given a campus to create, twenty-one buildings in all, as the Armour Institute merged with the Lewis Institute to form the Illinois Institute of Technology. Twenty-one large buildings, in the middle of the Depression, at a time when building had come almost to a halt in the United States—for an architect who had completed only seventeen buildings in his career—

O white gods.

Such prostrations! Such acts of homage! The Museum of Modern Art honored Gropius with a show called "Bauhaus: 1919–1928," those being the years

Ludwig Mies van der Rohe. White God No. 2. He put half of America inside German worker-housing cubes.

when Gropius headed it. Philip Johnson, now thirty-four years old, could resist the physical presence of the gods no longer. He decamped to Harvard to study to become an architect at Gropius' feet. Starting from zero! (If the truth be known, he would have preferred to be at Mies' feet, but to a supremely urbane young man like Johnson, we may be sure, the thought of moving to Chicago, Illinois, for three years was a bit more zero than he had in mind.)

It was embarrassing, perhaps . . . but it was the kind of thing one could learn to live with. . . . Within three years the course of American architecture had changed, utterly. It was not so much the buildings the

Germans designed in the United States, although Mies' were to become highly influential a decade later. It was more the system of instruction they introduced. Still more, it was *their very presence*. The most fabled creatures in all the mythology of twentieth-century American art—namely, those dazzling European artists poised so exquisitely against the rubble—they were . . . *here!* . . . *now!* . . . in the land of the colonial complex . . . to govern, in person, their big little Nigeria of the Arts.

This curious phase of late colonial history was by no means confined to architecture, for the colonial complex was all-pervasive. Stars of the two great rival movements of European painting, the Cubists and Surrealists, began arriving as refugees in the late 1930s and early 1940s. Léger, Mondrian, Modigliani, Chagall, Max Ernst, André Breton, Yves Tanguy—*O white gods!* The American Scene and Social Realist painting of the 1930s vanished, never to reappear. From the Europeans, artists in New York learned how to create their own clerisy. The first American art compound, the so-called New York School of abstract expressionists, was formed in the 1940s, with regular meetings, manifestos, new theories, new visual codes, the lot. Arnold Schoenberg, the white god of all the white gods in European music, arrived as a refugee in 1936. For the next forty years, serious music in America became a footnote to Schoenberg's theory of serial composition. There was considerable irony here. Many European composers looked to American jazz and to American composers such as George Gershwin, Aaron Copland, and Ferde Grofé as liberating forces, a way out of the hyper-rationalization of European avant-garde music as typified by Schoenberg. But serious American composers, by and large, were having none of that. They acted like Saudis being told their tents were marvelous because they were so natural and indigenous and earthy. They wanted the real thing—the European thing—and they fastened onto it with a vengeance. Thereafter, Gershwin, Copland, and Grofé were spoken of with condescension or else plain derision.*

In architecture, naturally, the Silver Prince became the chief executive, the governor of the colony, as it were. The teaching of architecture at Harvard was transformed overnight. Everyone started from zero. Everyone was now taught in the fundamentals of the International—which is to say, the compound—Style. All architecture became nonbourgeois architecture, although the concept itself was left discreetly *unexpressed,* as it were. The old Beaux-Arts traditions became heresy, and so did the legacy of Frank Lloyd Wright, which had only barely made its way into the architecture schools in the first place. Within three years, every so-called major American contribution to contemporary architecture—whether by Wright, H. H. Richardson, creator of the heavily rusticated American Romanesque, or Louis Sullivan, leader of the "Chicago School" of skyscraper architects— had dropped down into the footnotes, into the *ibid.* thickets.

Wright himself was furious and, for one of the few times in his life, bewildered. It was hard to say what

---

*Likewise, in the field of psychology. So many leading Freudian psychoanalysts came to the United States (e.g., Heinz Hartmann and Ernst Kris), the United States became the only important center of Freudian psychology in the world. American contributions to psychology, even those well regarded in Europe, such as William James's, were for the next forty years regarded as backward.

got under his skin more: the fact that his work had been upstaged by the Europeans or the fact that he was now treated as a species of walking dead man. He was not deprived of honor and respect, but when he got it, it often sounded like a memorial service. For example, the Museum of Modern Art put on an exhibition of Wright's work in 1940—but it was in tandem with a show of the work of the movie director D. W. Griffith, who had retired in 1931. Mies made a very gracious statement about what a genius Wright was and how he had opened up the eyes of European architects . . . back before the First World War . . . As to just what debt he might have felt to the eighty-odd buildings Wright had designed since then, he didn't say.

The late 1920s and early 1930s had been disastrous for Wright. He was already fifty-eight when a fire destroyed his studio at Taliesin, Wisconsin, in 1925. Troubles with his mistress, Miriam Noel, seemed to paralyze his practice. His business had fallen off badly even before the Depression. Wright had finally holed up, like a White Russian on his uppers, in his rebuilt redoubt at Taliesin, with a dozen or so apprentices, known as the Taliesin Fellows, his porkpie hats, berets, high collars and flowing neckties, and his capes from Stevenson, the Chicago tailor. Wright himself had been an apprentice of Louis Sullivan and had broken with or been fired by him—each had his own version—but Wright had taken with him Sullivan's vision of a totally new and totally American architecture, arising from the American terrain and the spirit of the Middle West. Well, now, finally, in the late 1930s, there was a totally new architecture in America, and it had come straight from Germany, Holland, and France, the French component being Le Corbusier.

Frank Lloyd Wright's Robie House, Chicago, 1906. Exemplar of his Prairie Style and his dream of a totally American architecture. Dream on, dream on . . .

Every time Wright read that Le Corbusier had finished a building, he told the Fellows: "Well, now that he's finished one building, he'll go write four books about it." Le Corbusier made one visit to the United States—and developed a phobia toward America—and Wright developed a phobia toward Le Corbusier. He turned down his one chance to meet him. He didn't want to have to shake his hand. As for Gropius, Wright always referred to him as "Herr Gropius." He didn't want to shake his hand, either. One day Wright made a surprise visit to a site in Racine, Wisconsin, where the first of his "Usonian" houses, medium-priced versions of his Prairie School manor houses, was going up. Wright's red Lincoln Zephyr pulled up to the front. One of his apprentices, Edgar Tafel, was at the wheel, serving as chauffeur. Just then, a group of men emerged from the building.

Among them was none other than Gropius himself, who had come to the University of Wisconsin to lecture and was anxious to see some of Wright's work. Gropius came over and put his face at the window and said, "Mr. Wright, it's a pleasure to meet you. I have always admired your work." Wright did not so much as smile or raise his hand. He merely turned his head ever so slightly toward the face at the window and said out of the side of his mouth, "Herr Gropius, you're a guest of the university here. I just want to tell you that they're as snobbish here as they are at Harvard, only they don't have a New England accent." Whereupon he turned to Tafel and said, "Well, we have to get on, Edgar!" And he settled back, and the red Zephyr sped off, leaving Gropius and entourage teetering on the edge of the curb with sunbeams shining through their ears.*

One up for Daddy Frank!—as the Fellows called Wright, when he was out of earshot. But it was one-upmanship of a hollow sort. Daddy Frank had just seen the face of the German who had replaced him as the Future of American Architecture.

Tafel and the other Fellows were Wright's only followers by now. Among the architecture students in the universities the International Style was all you heard about. Enthusiasm had been building up ever since the pilgrims had returned from Europe and the Museum of Modern Art began touting the compound architects. When the white gods suddenly arrived, enthusiasm became conversion, in the religious sense. There was a zeal about it that went quite beyond the ordinary passions of aesthetic taste. It was the esoteric,

---

*Edgar Tafel, *Apprentice to Genius: Years with Frank Lloyd Wright* (New York: McGraw-Hill Book Company, 1979).

Frank Lloyd Wright, circa 1935. He looked into the future of American architecture—and saw Walter Gropius' face. He was not pleased.

hierophantic fervor of the compound that seized them all. "Henceforth, the divinity of art and the authority of taste reside *here with us . . ."* The university architecture departments themselves became the American version of the compounds. Here was an approach to architecture that turned the American architect from a purveyor to bond salesmen to an engineer of the soul. With the Depression on, the bond salesmen weren't doing much for the architecture business anyway. New building had come to almost a dead halt. This made it even easier for the architectural community to take to the white gods' theories of starting from zero.

Studying architecture was no longer a matter of acquiring a set of technical skills and a knowledge of aesthetic alternatives. Before he knew it, the student found himself drawn into a movement and entrusted with a set of inviolable aesthetic and moral principles. The campus itself became the physical compound, as at the Bauhaus. When students talked about architecture, it was with a sense of mission. The American campus compounds differed one from the other—to an ever so slight degree, just as de Stijl differed from Bauhaus. Harvard was pure Bauhaus. At Yale they would experiment with variations. At one point the principle of "the integrally jointed wooden frame" seemed exhilaratingly rebellious—but it would have taken the superfine mind of Doctor Subtilis himself to have explained why. This, too, was after the manner of the European compounds.

Faculty members resisted the compound passion at their peril. Students were becoming unruly. They were drawing up petitions—manifestos in embryo. No more laying down laborious washes in china ink in the old Beaux-Arts manner! No more tedious Renaissance renderings! After all, look at Mies' drawings. He used no shading at all, just quick crisp straight lines, clean and to the point. And look at Corbu's! His draftsmanship—a veritable scribble! A pellmell rush of ideas! His renderings were watercolors in mauve and brown tones, as fast and terribly beautiful as a storm! Genius!—you had to let it *gush out!* We declare: No more stone-grinding classical Renaissance details!— and the faculties caved in. By 1940, the sketchiness of Corbu's quivering umber bird had become the modern standard for draftsmanship. With the somewhat grisly euphoria of Savonarola burning the wigs and fancy dresses of the Florentine fleshpots, deans of architecture went about instructing the janitors to throw out all plaster casts of classical details, pedagogical props that had been accumulated over a half century or more. I mean, my God, all those Esquiline vase-fountains and Temple of Vesta capitals . . . How very bourgeois.

At Yale, in the annual design competition, a jury always picked out one student as, in effect, best in show. But now the students rebelled. And why? Because it was written, in the scriptures, by Gropius himself: "The fundamental pedagogical mistake of the academy arose from its preoccupation with the idea of individual genius." Gropius' and Mies' byword was "team" effort. Gropius' own firm in Cambridge was not called Walter Gropius & Associates, Inc., or anything close to it. It was called "The Architects Collaborative." At Yale the students insisted on a group project, a collaborative design, to replace the obscene scramble for individual glory.

Now, in the late 1940s and early 1950s, Buckminster Fuller came into his own. Fuller was an American designer with an endless stock of ingenious notions, one of which was his geodesic dome, a dome created of thousands of short, thin metal struts arranged in tetrahedra. Fuller's dome fit in nicely with the modern principle of creating large structures with light surfaces out of machine-made materials and using tensions and stresses to do the work that massive supports had done for the old (bourgeois) order. But Gropius and the others never felt very comfortable with Fuller. It was hard to tell whether he was an architect, an engineer, a guru, or simply that species of nut known all around the world: *the inventor*. But to American university students he was a guru at the very least. He would give amazing twelve-hour lectures, great seamless geodesic domes of words that youths with supple spines and good kidneys found uplifting, even intoxicating. At Yale, after one of Fuller's amazing performances, the architecture students were swept up into an ecstasy of rebellious and collaborative action. They constructed an enormous geodesic dome of cardboard struts and put it up on top of Yale's stony gray Gothic Revival architecture school building, Weir Hall, and as much as dared the dean of architecture to try to do anything about it. He didn't, and the dome slowly rotted in its eminence.

In 1950, Yale got its own Bauhäusler when Josef Albers arrived from North Carolina to become the head of fine-arts instruction. Albers immediately instituted the fabled Bauhaus Vorkurs, except that now he wasn't interested in depositing sheets of newspaper on the table. Now he deposited squares of Color-aid paper on the table and told the students to create works of art. As a painter, Albers himself had spent the preceding fourteen years seeking to solve the problem (if any) of superimposing squares of color, one upon the other. Now he had the Yale students doing it . . . and month after month went by. Yale, simply because it was Yale, attracted outstanding artists from high schools all over America. Some young lad who could take a piece of marble and carve you a pillow that looked so full of voluptuous downy billows you would have willingly tried to bury your head in it—this reincarnation of Bernini himself would sit there with Albers' implacable Color-aid paper in his hands . . . *starting from zero* . . . and watch Albers point to some gristle-brained photographer's little playpretty layers of colored squares and hear him say: "But *this!*—is

form sculpted by light!" And the walls of the compound box closed in yet a few more inches.

As for the compound taboos concerning what was
bourgeois and nonbourgeois, these soon became the
very central nervous system of architecture students
in the universities, as if they had been encoded in their
genes. There was a bizarre story in the press at the
time about a drunk who had put a gun to the head of an
upland Tennessee foot-washing Baptist and ordered
him to utter a vile imprecation regarding Jesus Christ.
The victim was in no mood to be a martyr; in fact, he
desperately wished to save his own hide. But he was a
true believer, and *he could not make the words pass
his lips,* try as he might, and his brains were blown out.
So it was with the new generation of architects by the
late 1940s. There was *no circumstance* under which a
client could have prevailed upon them to incorporate
hipped roofs or Italianate cornices or broken pediments or fluted columns or eyebrow lintels or any of
the rest of the bourgeois baggage into their designs.
Try as they might, they could not make the drafting
pencil describe such forms.

O white gods.

An intellectual weakness—and saving grace—of
American students has always been that they are un
able to sit still for ideology and its tight flemish-bonded
logics and dialectics. They don't want it and don't get
it. Any possible connection that worker housing or
antibourgeois ideals might have had with a political
program, in Germany, Holland, or anywhere else,
eluded them. They picked up the sentimental side of it
only. I can remember what brave plans young architects at Yale and Harvard had for the common man
in the early 1950s. That was the term they used, *the
common man.* They had a vague notion that the common man was a workingman, and not an advertising

account executive, but beyond that it was all Trilby and Dickens. They were designing things for the common man down to truly minute details, such as lamp switches. The new liberated common man would live as the Cultivated Ascetic. He would be modeled on the B.A.-degree Greenwich Village bohemian of the late 1940s—dark wool Hudson Bay shirts, tweed jackets, flannel pants, briarwood pipes, sandals & simplicity— except that he would live in an enormous hive of glass and steel, i.e., an International Style housing project with elevators, instead of a fourth-floor walkup in a brownstone. So much for ideology. But the design side of the compounds they comprehended in all its reductionist, stereotaxic-needle-implant fineness. At Yale the students gradually began to notice that everything they designed, everything the faculty members designed, everything that the visiting critics (who gave critiques of student designs) designed . . . looked the same. Everyone designed the same . . . box . . . of glass and steel and concrete, with tiny beige bricks substituted occasionally. This became known as The Yale Box. Ironic drawings of The Yale Box began appearing on bulletin boards. "The Yale Box in the Mojave Desert"—and there would be a picture of The Yale Box out amid the sagebrush and the joshua trees northeast of Palmdale, California. "The Yale Box Visits Winnie the Pooh"—and there would be a picture of the glass-and-steel cube up in a tree, the child's treehouse of the future. "The Yale Box Searches for Captain Nemo"—and there would be a picture of The Yale Box twenty thousand leagues under the sea with a periscope on top and a propeller in back. There was something gloriously nutty about this business of The Yale Box!—but nothing changed. Even in serious moments, nobody could design anything *but* Yale Boxes.

The truth was that by now architectural students all over America were inside that very box, the same box the compound architects had closed in upon themselves in Europe twenty years before.

Every young architect's apartment, and every architecture student's room, was that box and that shrine. And in that shrine was always the same icon. I can still see it. The living room would be a mean little space on the backside of a walkup tenement. The couch would be a mattress on top of a flush door supported by bricks and covered with a piece of monk's cloth. There would be more monk's cloth used as curtains and on the floor would be a sisal rug that left corduroy ribs on the bottoms of your feet in the morning. The place would be lit by clamp-on heat lamps with half-globe aluminum reflectors and ordinary bulbs replacing the heat bulbs. At one end of the rug, there it would be . . . *the Barcelona chair.* Mies had designed it for his German Pavilion at the Barcelona Exposition of 1929. The Platonic ideal of *chair* it was, pure Worker Housing leather and stainless steel, the most perfect piece of furniture design in the twentieth century. The Barcelona chair commanded the staggering price of $550, however, and that was wholesale. When you saw that holy object on the sisal rug, you knew you were in a household where a fledgling architect and his young wife had sacrificed everything to bring the symbol of the godly mission into their home. Five hundred and fifty dollars! She had even given up the diaper service and was doing the diapers by hand. It got to the point where, if I saw a Barcelona chair, no matter where, I immediately—in the classic stimulus-response bond—smelled diapers gone high.

But if they already had the chair, why was she still doing the diapers by hand? Because one chair was only halfway to Mecca. Mies always used them in pairs. The state of grace, the Radiant City, was two Barcelona chairs, one on either end of the sisal rug, before the flush-door couch, under the light of the heat-lamp reflectors.

If a young man had suffered and sacrificed in this way and stripped the fat from his mental life and revealed the Mazda gleam at the apex of his soul—who, in the mundane world outside, could stop him now?

It was about this time, the late 1940s and early 1950s, that The Client in America began to realize that something very strange had taken place among the architects. At Yale the first of the rude jolts—many more would follow—came in 1953 with an addition to the Yale Art Gallery. Barely ten years before, on the eve of the Second World War, Yale had completed a building program of vast proportions that had turned the campus into as close an approximation of Oxford and Cambridge as the mind of man could devise on short notice in southern Connecticut. Edward Harkness, a partner of John D. Rockefeller, and John Sterling, who had a railroad fortune, donated most of the money. Eighteen medieval fortresses rose up, tower upon tower, in High Collegiate Gothic, to house ten residential colleges (Yale Mid-Atlantic for dormitories), four graduate schools, a library, a power plant, whose buttressed smokestack reminded people of the Cathedral at Rheims, a ten-story gymnasium known as the Cathedral of Sweat, and the twenty-one-story Harkness Tower, which had a carillon on top. All these soaring structures had rusticated stone façades. Gothic Revivalism was carried to the point not only of putting leaded panes in the casement windows but also of having craftsmen blow, etch, and stain panes with medieval designs, many of them detailed representa-

The Yale University Art Gallery. Original building (right) by Egerton Swartwout in 1928. Addition (left) by Louis Kahn twenty-five years later.

tions of religious figures and mythical animals, and installing them at seemingly random intervals. The result was a campus almost as unified, architecturally, as Jefferson's University of Virginia. For better or worse, Yale became the business barons' vision of a luxurious collegium for the sons of the upper classes who would run the new American empire.

The art-gallery addition, at York and Chapel Streets in New Haven, was Yale's first major building project following the Second World War. A gray little man named Louis Kahn was appointed as architect. His main recommendation seemed to be that he was a friend of the chairman of the architecture department,

George Howe. The existing gallery, built just twenty-five years earlier, was an Italian Romanesque palazzo designed by Egerton Swartwout, a Yale architect, and paid for by Harkness. It had massive cornices and a heavy pitched slate roof. On the Chapel Street side, it featured large windows framed in compound arches of stone.

Kahn's addition was . . . a box . . . of glass, steel, concrete, and tiny beige bricks. As his models and drawings made clear, on the Chapel Street side there would be no arches, no cornice, no rustication, no pitched roof—only a sheer blank wall of small glazed beige brick. The only details discernible on this slick and empty surface would be four narrow bands (string courses) of concrete at about ten-foot intervals. In the eyes of a man from Mars or your standard Yale man, the building could scarcely have been distinguished from a Woolco discount store in a shopping center. In the gallery's main public space the ceiling was made of gray concrete tetrahedra, fully exposed. This gave the interior the look of an underground parking garage.

Yale's administrators were shocked. Kahn had been an architect for twenty years but had done little more than work as assistant architect, under Howe, among others, on some housing projects. He was not much to look at, either, He was short. He had wispy reddish-white hair that stuck out this way and that. His face was badly scarred as the result of a childhood accident. He wore wrinkled shirts and black suits. The backs of his sleeves were shiny. He always had a little cigar of unfortunate hue in his mouth. His tie was always loose. He was nearsighted, and in the classrooms where he served as visiting critic, you would see Kahn holding some student's yard-long blueprint three inches from his face and moving his head over it like a scanner.

But that was merely the exterior. Somewhere deep within this shambles there seemed to be a molten core of confidence . . . and *architectural destiny* . . . Kahn would walk into a classroom, stare blearily at the students, open his mouth . . . and from the depths would come a remarkable voice:

"Every building must have . . . its own *soul*."

One day he walked into a classroom and began a lecture with the words: "Light . . . *is*." There followed a pause that seemed seven days long, just long enough to re-create the world.

His unlikely physical appearance only made these moments more striking. The visionary passion of the man was irresistible. Everybody was wiped out.

Kahn stared at the administrators in the same fashion, and the voice said: What do you mean, "It has nothing to do with the existing building"? You don't understand? You don't *see* it? You don't see the string courses? They express the floor lines of the existing building. They *reveal* the *structure*. For a quarter of a century, those floors have been hidden behind masonry, completely concealed. Now they will be *unconcealed*. Now the entire structure will be *unconcealed*. Honest form—*beauty,* as you choose to call it—can only result from *unconcealed structure!*

Unconcealed structure? Did he say *unconcealed structure?* Baffled but somehow intimidated, as if by Cagliostro or a Jacmel hoongan, the Yale administration yielded to the destiny of architecture and took it like a man.

Administrators, directors, boards of trustees, municipal committees, and executive officers have been taking it like men ever since.

4
Escape to Islip

HERE WE COME UPON one of the ironies of American life in the twentieth century. After all, this has been *the American century,* in the same way that the seventeenth might be regarded as the British century. This is the century in which America, the young giant, became the mightiest nation on earth, devising the means to obliterate the planet with a single device but also the means to escape to the stars and explore the rest of the universe. This is the century in which she became the richest nation in all of history, with a wealth that reached down to every level of the population. The energies and animal appetites and idle pleasures of even the working classes—the very term now seemed antique—became enormous, lurid, creamy, preposterous. The American family car was a 425-horsepower, twenty-two-foot-long Buick Electra with tail fins in back and two black rubber breasts on the bumper in front. The American liquor-store delivery-man's or cargo humper's vacation was two weeks in Barbados with his third wife or his new cookie. The

American industrial convention was a gin-blind rout at a municipal coliseum the size of all Rome, featuring vans in the parking lot stocked with hookers on flokati rugs for the exclusive use of registered members of the association. The way Americans lived made the rest of mankind stare with envy or disgust but always with awe. In short, this has been America's period of full-blooded, go-to-hell, belly-rubbing wahoo-yahoo youthful rampage—and what architecture has she to show for it? An architecture whose tenets prohibit every manifestation of exuberance, power, empire, grandeur, or even high spirits and playfulness, as the height of bad taste.

We brace for a barbaric yawp over the roofs of the world—and hear a cough at a concert.

In short, the reigning architectural style in this, the very Babylon of capitalism, became worker housing. Worker housing, as developed by a handful of architects, inside the compounds, amid the rubble of Europe in the early 1920s, was now pitched up high and wide, in the form of Ivy League art-gallery annexes, museums for art patrons, apartments for the rich, corporate headquarters, city halls, country estates. It was made to serve every purpose, in fact, except housing for workers.

It was not that worker housing was never built for workers. In the 1950s and early 1960s the federal government helped finance the American version of the Dutch and German Siedlungen of the 1920s. Here they were called public housing projects. But somehow the workers, intellectually undeveloped as they were, managed to avoid public housing. They called it, simply, "the projects," and they avoided it as if it had a smell. The workers—if by workers we mean people who have jobs—headed out instead to the suburbs.

They ended up in places like Islip, Long Island, and the San Fernando Valley of Los Angeles, and they bought houses with pitched roofs and shingles and clapboard siding, with no structure expressed if there was any way around it, with gaslight-style front-porch lamps and mailboxes set up on lengths of stiffened chain that seemed to defy gravity—the more cute and antiquey touches, the better—and they loaded these houses with "drapes" such as baffled all description and wall-to-wall carpet you could lose a shoe in, and they put barbecue pits and fishponds with concrete cherubs urinating into them on the lawn out back, and they parked the Buick Electras out front and had Evinrude cruisers up on tow trailers in the carport just beyond the breezeway.

As for the honest sculptural objects designed for worker-housing interiors, such as Mies' and Breuer's chairs, the proles either ignored them or held them in contempt because they were patently uncomfortable. This furniture is today a symbol of wealth and privilege, attuned chiefly to the tastes of the businessmen's wives who graze daily at the D & D Building, the major interior-decoration bazaar in New York. Mies' most famous piece of furniture design, the Barcelona chair, retails today for $3,465 and is available only through decorators. The high price is due in no small part to the chair's worker-housing honest non-bourgeois materials: stainless steel and leather. Today the leather can be ordered only in black or shades of brown. In the early 1970s, it seems, certain bourgeois elements were having them made in the most appalling variations . . . zebra skin, Holstein skin, ocelot skin, and *pretty fabrics*.*

---

*Robert Venturi, the architect, also ordered one in a pretty fabric in the interest of an "ironic reference."

The only people left trapped in worker housing in America today are those who don't work at all and are on welfare—these are the sole inhabitants of "the projects"—and, of course, the urban rich who live in places such as the Olympic Tower on Fifth Avenue in New York. Since the 1950s the term "luxury highrise" has come to denote a certain type of apartment house that is in fact nothing else but the Siedlungen of Frankfurt and Berlin, with units stacked up thirty, forty, fifty stories high, to be rented or sold to the bourgeoisie. Which is to say, pure nonbourgeois housing for the bourgeoisie only. Sometimes the towers are of steel, concrete, and glass; sometimes of glass, steel, and small glazed white or beige bricks. Always the ceilings are low, often under eight feet, the hallways are narrow, the rooms are narrow, even when they're long, the bedrooms are small (Le Corbusier was always in favor of that), the walls are thin, the doorways and windows have no casings, the joints have no moldings, the walls have no baseboards, and the windows don't open, although small vents or jalousies may be provided. The construction is invariably cheap in the pejorative as well as the literal sense. That builders could present these boxes in the 1950s, without a twitch of the nostril, as luxury, and that well-educated men and women could accept them, without a blink, as luxury—here is objective testimony, from those too dim for irony, to the aesthetic sway of the compound aesthetic, of the Silver Prince and his colonial legions, in America following the Second World War.

Every respected instrument of architectural opinion and cultivated taste, from *Domus* to *House & Garden,* told the urban dwellers of America that this was *living.* This was the good taste of today; this was modern, and soon the International Style became known simply as modern architecture. Every Sunday, in its design section, *The New York Times Magazine* ran a picture of the same sort of apartment. I began to think of it as *that apartment*. The walls were always pure white and free of moldings, casings, baseboards, and all the rest. In the living room there were about 17,000 watts' worth of R-40 spotlights encased in white canisters suspended from the ceiling in what is known as track lighting. There was always a set of bentwood chairs, blessed by Le Corbusier, which no one ever sat in because they caught you in the small of the back like a karate chop. The dining-room table was a smooth slab of blond wood (no ogee edges, no beading on the legs), around which was a set of the S-shaped, tubular steel, cane-bottomed chairs that Mies van der Rohe had designed—the second most famous chair designed in the twentieth century, his own Barcelona chair being first, but also one of the five most disastrously designed, so that by the time the main course arrived, at least one guest had pitched face forward into the lobster bisque. Somewhere nearby was a palm or a dracena fragrans or some other huge tropical plant, because all the furniture was so lean and clean and bare and spare that without some prodigious piece of frondose Victoriana from the nursery the place looked absolutely empty. The photographer always managed to place the plant in the foreground, so that the stark scene beyond was something one peered at through an arabesque of equatorial greenery. (And *that apartment* is still with us, every Sunday.)

So what if you were living in a building that looked like a factory and felt like a factory, and paying top dollar for it? Every modern building of quality looked like a factory. That was *the look of today*. You only had to think of Mies' campus for the Illinois Institute of Technology, most of which had gone up in the

1940s. The main classroom building looked like a shoe factory. The chapel looked like a power plant. The power plant itself, also designed by Mies, looked rather more spiritual (as Charles Jencks would point out), thanks to its chimney, which reached heavenward at least. The school of architecture building had black steel trusses rising up through the roof on either side of the main entrance, after the manner of a Los Angeles car wash. All four were glass and steel boxes. The truth was, this was inescapable. The compound style, with its *nonbourgeois* taboos, had so reduced the options of the true believer that every building, the beach house no less than the skyscraper, was bound to have the same general look.

And so what? The terms *glass box* and *repetitious,* first uttered as terms of opprobrium, became badges of honor. Mies had many American imitators, Philip Johnson, I. M. Pei, and Gordon Bunshaft being the most famous and the most blatant. And the most unashamed. Snipers would say that every one of Philip Johnson's buildings was an imitation of Mies van der Rohe. And Johnson would open his eyes wide and put on his marvelous smile of mock innocence and reply, "I have always been delighted to be called Mies van der Johnson." Bunshaft had designed Lever House, corporate headquarters for the Lever Brothers soap and detergent company, on Park Avenue. The building was such a success that it became the prototype for the American glass box, and Bunshaft and his firm, Skidmore, Owings & Merrill, did many variations on this same design. To the charge that glass boxes were all he designed, Bunshaft liked to crack: "Yes, and I'm going to keep on doing them until I do one I like."

For a hierophant of the compound, confidence came easy! What did it matter if they said you were imitating

Mies or Gropius or Corbu or any of the rest? It was like accusing a Christian of imitating Jesus Christ.

Mies' star had risen steadily since his arrival in the United States in 1938, due in no small part to the influence of Philip Johnson. Johnson had chosen Mies as one of the four great modernists in his "International Style" piece in 1932. He then helped arrange his emigration to America and his extraordinary job at the Armour Institute. In 1947, after most of Mies' campus buildings were underway, Johnson published the first book on his work. Mies was pushing sixty, but thanks to Johnson he had a glorious new career in America. With or without Johnson, however, Mies knew his way around in an era of art compounds. He had been director of architecture for the Novembergruppe back in 1919; he had founded the group's magazine, *G* (which stood for *Gestaltung,* meaning "creative force"); he had become a skilled propagandist with a flair for aphorisms. His most famous was "Less is more," to which he added: "My architecture is almost nothing." His idea was to combine the usual worker-housing elements in ways that were austere and elegant at the same time, along the lines of what today is called "minimalism." Mies himself was anything but austere. He was a big, beefy but handsome individual who smoked expensive cigars. Full coronas, they were. He looked rather like a Ruhr industrialist. He was also an affable soul, so much so that even Frank Lloyd Wright liked him. He was the one white god Wright could abide.

In 1958, the greatest single monument to the architecture of the Dutch and German compounds went up on Park Avenue, across the street from Lever House. This was the Seagram Building, designed by Mies himself, with Philip Johnson as his assistant. The

Seagram Building was worker housing, utterly non-bourgeois, pitched up thirty-eight stories on Park Avenue for the firm that manufactured a rye whiskey called Four Roses. In keeping with the color of the American whiskey bottle, the glass for this greatest of all boxes of glass and steel was tinted brownish amber. When it came to the exposed steel—well, since brownish steel didn't exist, except in a state of rust, bronze was chosen. Wasn't this adding a *color,* like poor Bruno Taut? No, bronze was bronze; that was the way it came, right out of the foundry. As for the glass, all glass ended up with a tint of some sort, usually greenish. Tinting it brown was only a machine-made tint control. Right? (Besides, this was *Mies.*) Exposing the metal had presented a problem. Mies' vision of ultimate nonbourgeois purity was a building composed of nothing but steel beams and glass, with concrete slabs creating the ceilings and floors. But now that he was in the United States he ran into American building and fire codes. Steel was terrific for tall buildings because it could withstand great lateral stresses as well as support great weights. Its weakness was that the heat of a fire could cause steel to buckle. American codes required that structural steel members be encased in concrete or some other fireproof material. That slowed Mies up for only a little while. He had already worked it out in Chicago, in his Lake Shore apartment buildings. What you did was enclose the steel members in concrete, as required, and then reveal them, *express* them, by sticking vertical wide-flange beams on the outside of the concrete, as if to say: "Look! Here's what's inside." But sticking things on the outside of the buildings . . . Wasn't that exactly what was known, in another era, as applied decoration? Was there any way you could call such a thing *functional?* No prob-

Left: Gordon Bunshaft's Lever House, the mother of all the glass boxes. She was as fecund as the shad. Bottom right: The Seagram Building. Mies pitches worker housing up thirty-eight stories, and capitalists use it as corporate headquarters. Note the curtains and blinds: only three positions allowed—up, down, and halfway. Top right: Corner of the Seagram Building. Custom-made bronze wide-flange beams stuck on the exterior to "express" the real ones concealed beneath the concrete of the pier.

lem. At the heart of functional, as everyone knew, was not *function* but the spiritual quality known as *nonbourgeois*. And what could be more nonbourgeois than an unadorned wide-flange beam, straight out of the mitts of a construction worker?

The one remaining problem was window coverings: shades, blinds, curtains, whatever. Mies would have preferred that the great windows of plate glass have no coverings at all. Unless you could compel everyone in a building to have the same color ones (white or beige, naturally) and raise them and lower them or open and shut them at the same time and to the same degree, they always ruined the purity of the design of the exterior. In the Seagram Building, Mies came as close as man was likely to come to realizing that ideal. The tenant could only have white blinds or shades, and there were only three intervals where they would stay put: open, closed, and halfway. At any other point, they just kept sliding.

No intellectually undeveloped impulses, please. By now this had become a standard attitude among compound architects in America. They policed the impulses of clients and tenants alike. Even after the building was up and the contract fulfilled, they would return. The imitators of Le Corbusier—and there were many—would build expensive country houses in wooded glades patterned on Corbu's Villa Savoye, with strict instructions that the bedrooms, being on the upper floor and visible only to the birds, have no curtains whatsoever. Tired of waking up at 5 a.m. every morning to the light of the summer sun, the owners would add white curtains. But the soul engineer would inevitably return and rip the offending rags down . . . and throw out those sweet little puff 'n' clutter Thai-silk throw pillows in the living room while he was at it.

In the great corporate towers, the office workers shoved filing cabinets, desks, wastepaper baskets, potted plants, up against the floor-to-ceiling sheets of glass, anything to build a barrier against the panicked feeling that they were about to pitch headlong into the streets below. Above these jerry-built walls they strung up makeshift curtains that looked like laundry lines from the slums of Naples, anything to keep out that brain-boiling, poached-eye sunlight that came blazing in every afternoon . . . And by night the custodial staff, the Miesling police, under strictest orders, invaded and pulled down these pathetic barricades thrown up against the pure vision of the white gods and the Silver Prince. Eventually, everyone gave up and learned, like the haute bourgeoisie above him, to take it like a man.

They even learned to accept the Mieslings' two great pieces of circular reasoning. To those philistines who were still so gauche as to say that the new architecture lacked the richness of detail of the old Beaux-Arts architecture, the plasterwork, the metalwork, the masonry, and so on, the Mieslings would say with considerable condescension: "Fine. You produce the craftsmen who can do that kind of work, and then we'll talk to you about it. They don't exist anymore." True enough. But why? Henry Hope Reed tells of riding across West Fifty-third Street in New York in the 1940s in a car with some employees of E. F. Caldwell & Co., a firm that specialized in bronze work and electrical fixtures. As the car passed the Museum of Modern Art building, the men began shaking their fists at it and shouting: "That goddamn place is destroying us! Those bastards are killing us!" In the palmy days of Beaux-Arts architecture, Caldwell had employed a thousand bronzeurs, marble workers, model makers, and designers. Now the company was sliding into insolvency, along with many similar firms. It was not that craftsmanship was dying. Rather, the International Style was finishing off the demand for it, particularly in commercial construction. By the same token, to those who complained that International Style buildings were cramped, had flimsy walls inside as well as out, and, in general, looked cheap, the knowing response was: "These days it's too expensive to build in any other style." But it was not *too* expensive, merely *more* expensive. The critical point was what people would or would not put up with aesthetically. It was possible to build in styles even cheaper than the International Style. For example, England began to experiment with schools and public housing constructed like airplane hangars, out of corrugated metal tethered by guy wires. Their architects also said: "These days it's too expensive to build in any other style." Perhaps one day soon everyone *(tout le monde)* would learn to take this, too, like a man.

The Selection Committee stood by at all times, to aid in the process. The day of the monarch such as Ludwig II of Bavaria, or the business autocrat such as Herbert F. Johnson of Johnson Wax, who personally selected architects for great public buildings was over. Governments and corporations now turned to the selection committee. And the selection committee typically included at least one prestigious architect, who, being prestigious, was of course a product of the compounds. And as the baffling and forbidding plans came in, from other compound architects, the various directors and executive officers on the committee turned, nonplussed, to the architect, and he assured them: "These days it's too expensive to build in any other style." And: "Fine. You produce the craftsmen,

and then we'll talk to you about it." And the circle
closed once and for all. And the mightiest of the
mighty learned to take it like a man.

Not even the bottom dogs, those on welfare, trapped
in the projects, have taken it so supinely. The lumpen-
proles have fought it out with the legions of the Silver
Prince, and they have won a battle or two. In 1955 a
vast worker-housing project called Pruitt-Igoe was
opened in St. Louis. The design, by Minoru Yamasaki,
architect of the World Trade Center, won an award
from the American Institute of Architects. Yamasaki
designed it classically Corbu, fulfilling the master's vision of highrise hives of steel, glass, and concrete
separated by open spaces of green lawn. The workers
of St. Louis, of course, were in no danger of getting
caught in Pruitt-Igoe. They had already decamped for
suburbs such as Spanish Lake and Crestwood. Pruitt-
Igoe filled up mainly with recent migrants from the
rural South. They moved from areas of America where
the population density was fifteen to twenty folks per
square mile, where one rarely got more than ten feet
off the ground except by climbing a tree, into Pruitt-
Igoe's fourteen-story blocks.

On each floor there were covered walkways, in
keeping with Corbu's idea of "streets in the air." Since
there was no other place in the project in which to *sin*
in public, whatever might ordinarily have taken place
in bars, brothels, social clubs, pool halls, amusement
arcades, general stores, corncribs, rutabaga patches,
hayricks, barn stalls, now took place in the streets in
the air. Corbu's boulevards made Hogarth's Gin Lane
look like the oceanside street of dreams in Southamp-
ton, New York. Respectable folk pulled out, even if it
meant living in cracks in the sidewalks. Millions of

The Pruitt-Igoe projects, St. Louis, July 15, 1972. Mankind finally arrives at a workable solution to the problem of public housing.

dollars and scores of commission meetings and task-force projects were expended in a last-ditch attempt to make Pruitt-Igoe habitable. In 1971, the final task force called a general meeting of everyone still living in the project. They asked the residents for their suggestions. It was a historic moment for two reasons. One, for the first time in the fifty-year history of worker housing, someone had finally asked the client for his two cents' worth. Two, the chant. The chant began immediately: "Blow it . . . *up!* Blow it . . . *up!* Blow it . . . *up!* Blow it . . . *up!* Blow it . . . *up!*" The next day the task force thought it over. The poor buggers were right. It was the only solution. In July of 1972, the city blew up the three central blocks of Pruitt-Igoe with dynamite.

That part of the worker-housing saga has not ended. It has just begun. At almost the same time that Pruitt-Igoe went down, the Oriental Gardens project went up in New Haven, the model city of urban renewal in America. The architect was one of America's most prestigious compound architects, Paul Rudolph, dean of the Yale School of Architecture. The federal government's Department of Housing and Urban Development, which was paying for the project, hailed Rudolph's daring design as the vision of the housing projects of the future. The Oriental Gardens were made of clusters of prefabricated modules. You would never end up with more disadvantaged people than you bargained for. You could keep adding modules and clustering the poor yobboes up until they reached Bridgeport. The problem was that the modules didn't fit together too well. In through the cracks came the cold and the rain. Out the doors, the ones that still opened, went whatever respectable folks had gone in in the first place. By September of 1980 there were only seventeen tenants left. Early in 1981, HUD itself set about demolishing it.

Other American monuments to 1920s Middle European worker housing began falling down of their own accord. These were huge sports arenas and convention centers, such as the Hartford Civic Center coliseum, which had flat roofs. The snow was too much for them—but they collapsed piously, paying homage on the way down to the dictum that pitched roofs were bourgeois.

5
The Apostates

AS HE TOLD the story, Edward Durell Stone, one of the earliest of the International Style architects in America, boarded an airplane from New York to Paris one night in 1953 and found himself sitting next to a woman named Maria Elena Torchio. Her father was an Italian architect; her mother was from Barcelona; and Maria, Stone liked to say, was "explosively Latin." He fell in love with her over the Atlantic and proposed to her over the English Channel. She didn't fall so fast. For a start, she thought his clothes looked like a college professor's. She wasn't wild about his buildings, either. Very careful buildings, they were, very restrained, a bit cold, a bit lifeless, if the truth were known . . . not very explosively Latin . . .

In 1954 Stone married Maria Elena Torchio and changed his style completely and created the luxurious and ornamental design of the American Embassy in New Delhi, with its terrazzo grilles of concrete and marble, its steel columns finished with gold leaf, its water garden traversed by curvilinear islands, isles, and islets. He thought of the embassy as his "Taj Maria." What happened to Stone in the architectural world after the unveiling of the Taj—*gold leaf?*—gives us a picture of the other side of compound passion. It shows us the fate of the apostate.

Stone was the man who had designed the first International Style house built on the East Coast, the Mandel House in Mount Kisco, New York, in 1933. (An Austrian emigré, Richard Neutra, had built one in Los Angeles, the Lovell House, in 1928.) In 1934 Stone built his second International Style house in Mount Kisco, the Kowalski House, and the community rose up and changed the local building codes to put an end to the baffling infestation. So far, so good; a little flushing out of the philistines served one well in the compound. Stone's credentials were so impeccable, in fact, that the Museum of Modern Art chose him as architect, along with Philip L. Goodwin, for its building on West Fifty-third Street, just off Fifth Avenue, on a site where the townhouses of both John D. Rockefeller, Jr., and John D. Himself had stood. Here would be the museum's own exemplary building to show all New York the International Style. Stone had been chosen to devise the object lesson, the very flagship, of Utopia, Ltd.

The moment the New Delhi embassy was unveiled, Stone was dropped like an embezzler by *le monde* of fashionable architecture, which is to say, the university-based world of the European compounds. *Gold* here and *luxurious* there and *marbled* and *curvilinear* everywhere . . . How very bour— No, it was *bourgeois ne plus ultra.* There was no way that even Mies himself, master of the bronze wide-flange beam,

The Two Stones. 1939: Edward Durell Stone, true believer, does the Museum of Modern Art's building (left). 1964: Edward Durell Stone, apostate, does Huntington Hartford's Gallery of Modern Art. "Marble Lollipops!" screamed the true believers.

could have argued his way out of a production like this one. What made it more galling was that Stone didn't even try. He kissed off the International Style. To critics of his Kennedy Center in Washington, a vastly enlarged version of his Taj Maria, Stone retorted that it represented "twenty-five hundred years of Western culture rather than twenty-five years of modern architecture." The man was not even a backslider. He was an apostate pure and simple. He had renounced the fundamental principles.

The fate of the apostate, classically, is that curse known as anathema. Within the world of architecture, among those in a position to build or dismantle reputations, every building Stone did thereafter was buried in anathematism. When the Museum of Modern Art decided to build an addition on West Fifty-third Street, there was not one chance in a thousand that Stone was going to be chosen to add to his own building. The job went to the most fashionable of all the American compound architects, Philip Johnson, now a graduate of the Harvard school of architecture, albeit still at the feet of the Silver Prince. In one of American art history's nicer turns of plot, Stone was chosen instead by Huntington Hartford to design his Gallery of Modern Art nine blocks away at Columbus Circle. Hartford was a maverick on the art scene, a collector of the Pre-Raphaelites and Salvador Dali, to mention but two of his unfashionable tastes. He was building his museum specifically to challenge Utopia, Ltd., and all its works.-I can remember vividly the automatic sniggers, the rolling of the eyeballs, that mention of Stone's building for Hartford set off at that time. The reviews of the architectural critics were bad enough. But not even such terms as "Kitsch for the rich" and "Marble Lollipops" convey the poisonous mental atmosphere

in which Stone now found himself. He was reduced, at
length, to saying things such as, "Every taxi driver in
New York will tell you it's his favorite building." After
so much! after a lifetime!—to be hounded, finally, to
the last populist refuge of a Mickey Spillane or a Jac-
queline Susann . . . O Lord! *Anathema!*

One will note that Stone's business did not collapse
following his apostasy, merely his prestige. The Taj
Maria did wonders for his practice in a commercial
sense. After all, the International Style was well hated
even by those who commissioned it. There were still
others ready to go to considerable lengths not to have
to deal with it in the first place. They were happy
enough to find an architect with modernist credentials,
even if they had lapsed, who was willing to give them
something else. But in terms of his reputation within
the fraternity, Stone was poison. He was beyond serious consideration. He had removed himself from the
court. He was out of the game.

Eero Saarinen's experience was similar, although
the hostility was not nearly so virulent. Saarinen was
of noble modernist-architecture lineage. His father,
Eliel, was a Finnish architect often compared to the
Vienna Secessionists. Saarinen had been a conventional International Style architect until 1956, when he
designed the Trans World Airlines terminal at Idlewild
Airport (now Kennedy) in New York. The building
was made of the conventional materials, glass, steel,
and concrete, but it looked unmistakably like . . . an
eagle. His Dulles Airport building in Washington was
an even more flamboyant bird-in-flight sculpture with
pagoda overtones . . . His Ingalls ice-hockey rink at
Yale looked like a whale or a turtle. (Not the first
animals that ice hockey might bring to mind, but so be
it.) In Saarinen's case, the curvilinear shapes were the

The winged roof of Eero Saarinen's Dulles International Airport (top) and the eagle shape of his TWA terminal infuriated modernists. Originality in design had become a cardinal sin.

least of it. The man had lapsed into some sort of Hindu *zoömorphism*. Saarinen had decided to go his own way, in a frank bid to become the unique genius of twentieth-century architecture. He said he would like "a place in architectural history." He had picked the wrong era. There were geniuses in architecture, but they could not be unique. They had to be part of a compound, part of a "consensus," to use one of Mies' terms. The world of the compounds simply watched him disappear into the zoömorphic swamp mists. He was seldom attacked directly, the way Stone was. He was shut out from serious consideration, and that was that. I can remember writing a piece for the magazine *Architecture Canada* in which I mentioned Saarinen in terms that indicated the man was worthy of study. I ran into one of New York's best-known architectural writers at a party, and he took me aside for some fatherly advice.

"I enjoyed your piece," he said, "and I agreed with your point, in principle. But I have to tell you that you are only hurting your own cause if you use Saarinen as an example. People just won't take you seriously. I mean, *Saarinen* . . ."

I wish there were some way I could convey the look on his face. It was that cross between a sneer and a shrug that the French are so good at, the look that says the subject is so *outré*, so *infra dig*, so *de la boue*, one can't even spend time analyzing it without having some of the rubbish rub off.

The principle illustrated by the Saarinen case was: no architect could achieve a major reputation outside the compounds, which were now centered in the universities. The architect who insisted on going his own way stood no chance of being hailed as a pioneer of some important new direction. At best, he could hope to be regarded as an eccentric, like Saarinen or the Oklahoma architects Bruce Goff and Herbert Greene. (Oklahoma wasn't too terrific a vantage point in the first place.) At worst he would be the apostate, covered in anathema, like Stone.

Stone and Saarinen, like Frank Lloyd Wright and Goff and Greene, were *too American*, which meant both too parochial (not part of the International Style) and too bourgeois. Somehow they actually catered to the Hog-stomping Baroque exuberance of American civilization. When Stone designed the Kennedy Center in Washington with a lobby six stories high and six hundred and thirty feet long—so big, as one journalist pointed out, that Mickey Mantle's mightiest home run would have been just another long fly ball—it was regarded as an obscenity. Stone was actually playing *up* to American megalomania. He was *encouraging* the barbaric yawps. He was glorifying The Client's own grandiose sentiments.

It was difficult to say all this in so many words, of course. Hence the shrugs and *that look*, which still flourishes today. How else to deal with the barbaric yawps of the major hotel architects, such as Morris Lapidus and John Portman? Probably no architects ever worked harder to capture the spirit of American wealth and glamour after the Second World War than these two men: Lapidus, with his Americana and Eden Roc hotels in Miami Beach; Portman, with his Hyatts all across the country. Their work was so striking and so large in scale it was impossible for their fellow architects to ignore it. So they gave it *that look*. Portman received the shrug and that look. Lapidus received that look and a snigger.

Lapidus had started off his career in the theater and had gone to Columbia to study architecture, with the

idea of becoming a set designer. He wound up an architect. He had not been detained for even a moment
by debates over honest materials and unconcealed
structure. His vision remained theatrical from beginning to end. He had a Rimsky-Korsakov American
approach that was as thorough, as monolithic, in its
way as the Gropius approach in its way. When
Lapidus did a resort hotel, he designed everything,
down to the braid on the waiters' jackets, even though
the developers were seldom meticulous in carrying out
such details. His lobby for the Americana Hotel in
Miami Beach, with its tropical forest stuffed in a great
glass cone, haunch-to-paunch with a Two Weeks in
Florida version of the grand staircase at the Paris
Opéra—well, here was the lush life, postwar American, in a single great and gaudy image.

In 1970 Lapidus' work was selected as the subject of
an Architectural League of New York show and panel
discussion entitled "Morris Lapidus: Architecture of
Joy." Ordinarily this was an honor. In Lapidus' case it
was hard to say what it was. I was asked to be on the
panel—probably, as I look back on it, with the hope
that I might offer a "pop" perspective. (This word,
"pop," had already come to be one of the curses of my
life.) The evening took on an uneasy, rather camp atmosphere—uneasy, because Lapidus himself had
turned up in the audience. His work was being regarded not so much as architecture as a pop phenomenon, like Dick Tracy or the Busby Berkeley movies. I
kept trying to put in my two cents' worth about the
general question of portraying American power,
wealth, and exuberance in architectural form. I might
as well have been talking about numerology in the
Yucatán. The initial camp rush had passed, and the
assembled architects began to give Lapidus' work a
predictable going-over. At the end, Lapidus himself

stood up and said that the Soviets had once asked him to come to Russia and design some public housing and that they had been highly pleased with the results. Then he sat down. Nobody could quite figure it out, unless he was making a desperate claim of redeeming social significance . . . that might make him less radioactive in an architectural world given over to hotels, luxury highrises, schools, and corporate headquarters in the style of worker housing.

John Portman, meantime, has become the Lapidus of today. His enormous Babylonian ziggurat hotels, with their thirty-story atriums and hanging gardens and crystal elevators, have succeeded, more than any other sort of architecture, in establishing the look of Downtown, of Urban Glamour in the 1970s and 1980s. But within the university compounds—it is not so much that he is attacked . . . as that he does not *exist*. He is invisible. He takes on the uncertain contours of the folk architect. He becomes a highly commercial (and therefore unredeemable) version of Simon Rodia, who built the Watts Towers. What was a Hyatt Atrium Ziggurat, anyway, but a Watts Tower production with the assistance of mortgage brokers and automatic elevators?

Within the university compounds there was no way for an architect to gain prestige through an architecture that was wholly unique or specifically American in spirit. Not even Wright could do it—not even Wright, with the most prodigious outpouring of work in the history of American architecture. From 1928 to 1935, only two Wright buildings were constructed. But in 1935 he did Fallingwater, a home for Edgar J. Kaufmann, Sr., father of one of his apprentices. This structure of concrete slabs, anchored in rock and cantilevered out over a waterfall in the Pennsylvania high-

The atrium lobby of John Portman's Hyatt Regency O'Hare Hotel near O'Hare Airport, Chicago. Portman's American exuberance was more than the sons of the Silver Prince could stomach.

lands, was the start of the final phase of Wright's career. He was sixty-eight years old at the time. In the next twenty-three years, until his death at the age of ninety-one in 1959, he did more than half of his life's work, more than 180 buildings, including the Johnson Wax headquarters in Racine, Wisconsin, Herbert F. Johnson's mansion, Wingspread, Taliesin West, the Florida Southern campus, the Usonian homes, the Price Company Tower, and the Guggenheim Museum. Within the university compounds this earned Wright a reputation like Andrew Wyeth's in the world of painting: okay, for a back number.

In a way, the very productivity of a man like Wright, Portman, or Stone counted against him, given the new mental atmosphere in the universities. Oh, it was easy enough, one supposed, to go out into the marketplace and wheedle and vamp and dance for clients and get buildings to do. But the brave soul was he who remained within the compound, stayed within the university orbit, and risked the first ten or twenty years of his career in intellectual competition, doing the occasional small building, where a convenient opportunity presented itself, in the Corbu manner: a summer house for a friend, an addition to some faculty member's house, and—if all else failed—that old standby, the retirement home for Mother, which she paid for. It was no longer enough to build extraordinary buildings to show the world. The world could wait. It was now necessary to win in the competition that took place solely within and between the world of academic architecture.

For that matter, in most of the higher arts in America prestige was now determined by European-style clerisies. By the mid-1960s, painting was a truly advanced case. The Abstract Expressionists had held

on as the ruling compound for about ten years, but
then new theories, new compounds, new codes began
succeeding one another in a berserk rush. Pop Art, Op
Art, Minimalism, Hard Edge, Color Field, Earth Art,
Conceptual Art—the natural bias of the compounds
toward arcane and baffling went beyond all known
limits. The spectacle was crazy, but young artists
tended to believe—correctly—that it was impossible
to achieve major status without joining in the game. In
the field of serious music, the case was even more
advanced; in fact, it was very nearly terminal. Within
the university compounds, composers had become so
ultra-Schoenbergian, so exquisitely abstract, that no
one from the outside world any longer had the slightest
interest in, much less comprehension of, what was going on. In the cities, not even that Gideon's army
known as "the concert-going public" could be drawn
to an all-contemporary program. They took place only
in university concert halls. Here on the campus the
program begins with Scott Joplin's "Maple Leaf Rag,"
followed by one of Stockhausen's early compositions,
"Punkte," then Babbitt's Ensembles for Synthesizer, a
little Easley Blackwood and Jean Barraqué for a
change of pace, then the committed plunge into a ran-
dom-note or, as they say, "stochastic" piece for piano,
brass, Moog synthesizer, and computer by Iannis
Xenakis. The program winds up with James P. Johnson's "You Gotta Be Modernistic." Joplin and Johnson, of course, are as cozy and familiar as a lullaby,
but they are essential to the program. The same thirty-
five or forty souls, all of them faculty members and
graduate students, make up the audience at every contemporary musical event. The unspeakable fear is that
not even they will show up unless promised a piece of
candy at the beginning and a piece of candy at the end.

Joplin and Johnson numbers are okay because both men were black and were not appreciated as serious composers in their own day.

Choreographers had been slow in comprehending the idea of the compound, perhaps since dance had always seemed, by its very nature, representational. But by the 1960s they had made up for lost time. George Balanchine, the Russian choreographer who emigrated to the U.S. via Paris in 1934, was putting on abstract, neoclassical ballet at Lincoln Center by 1962. Choreographers such as Merce Cunningham and Yvonne Rainer set about removing all traces of sexuality from dance, even in the simple sense of male and female roles, all traces of narrative, scenery, and costume, even all traces of music as a source of dance tempo. In fact, people in all the arts seemed obsessed with creating clerisies, with baffling the bourgeoisie, no matter how unlikely the prospects. For example, photography had always seemed to be a form of expression with an implacable obviousness to it. But photographers and their theorists, such as John Szarkowski, curator of photography at Utopia, Ltd., began to find a way around this impediment. Hadn't Braque called for recognition of the fact that painting was nothing more than an arrangement of forms and colors on a flat surface? Which is to say, hadn't he made a virtue out of what had always seemed a shortcoming? Of course he had. So Szarkowski & Co. now made a virtue of what had always been regarded as photography's flaws: blurring, grotesque foreshortenings, untrue colors, images chopped off by the edge of the film frame, and so on. They achieved their goal; they managed to make photography utterly baffling to those unwilling to come inside the compound and learn the theories and the codes.

Clerisy! The compound! The codes! The new arcana! The European fashion proved irresistible. Even
among novelists. The strong suits of American fiction
in the twentieth century had been the realistic novel
and the realistic short story. The American realistic
novel of the 1930s had achieved considerable prestige
in Europe, precisely because of its rude animal vigor.
The American realists seemed as free and dionysian as
the jazz musicians. But by the late 1960s the most
talented young American writers in the universities—
and few new writers came from anywhere else—now
tended to look upon the realistic novel as a hopelessly
primitive and out-of-date form. They set about ex-
punging all realistic dialogue, local color, social issues,
or other slices of real life from their work. They sought
to write modern fables after the manner of the contemporary European masters, such as Kafka, Zamyatin,
and the playwrights Pinter and Beckett.

The twentieth century, the American century, was
now two-thirds over—and the colonial complex was
stronger than ever. Young philosophers in the universities were completely bowled over by the French
vogue   for   so-called   analytical   approaches   to
philosophy, such as Structuralism and Deconstructiv-
ism. The idea was that the old "idealistic" concerns of
nineteenth-century philosophy—God, Freedom, Im-
mortality, man's fate—were hopelessly naïve and
bourgeois. The proper concern of philosophy was the
nature of meaning. Which is to say, the proper concern
of philosophy was the arcana of the philosophical clerisy itself. In an era in which wars had become so all-
encompassing they were known as world wars—in
which people were now concentrated in metropolises
of a scale and complexity never before envisioned by
man—in which collisions of the races began to shake

the stability of the globe—in which man had usurped the godly power to plunge the world into destruction— in such an era, what was the overriding concern of American philosophers? Why, it was the same as that of the French philosophers whom they idolized. By day, Structuralists constructed the structure of meaning and pondered the meaning of structure. By night, Deconstructivists pulled the cortical edifice down. And the next day the Structuralists started in again . . .

O faithful colonial yeomen!

It was not necessary for even the most highly educated person to be troubled for very long by contemporary philosophy, painting, or music. In the case of music, it was obvious that he need not be troubled at all. But the case of architecture was quite different. There was no way whatsoever to avoid the fashions of the architectural compounds, no matter how esoteric they might become. In architecture, intellectual fashion was displayed fifty to a hundred stories high in the cities and in endless de Chirico vistas in the shopping malls of the new American suburbs.

O worker housing.

6

The Scholastics

AND WHAT ARCHITECT, here in the colony, fifty years later, was going to change things? What architect, as the Eagle screamed his supremacy in the twentieth century, dared design for America anything but homage to 1920s Middle European worker housing? To be fair about it, it was not merely a matter of daring, as the sad experience of Stone and Saarinen had shown. No, the only way to establish one's originality and be respected for it, was to proceed with infinite subtlety and with consummate respect for the proprieties. And never mind building buildings. The new way was first demonstrated in 1966 by a forty-one-year-old architect, Robert Venturi, who had built scarcely half a dozen buildings in his life.

Venturi published a book called *Complexity and Contradiction in Architecture* as part of a Museum of Modern Art series on "the theoretical background of modern architecture." Venturi's essay looked, on the face of it, like sheer apostasy. He took Mies' famous dictum, "Less is more," and turned it on its head. "Less is a bore," he said. He called for "messy vitality" to replace modernism's "obvious unity," for "hybrid" elements to replace modernism's "pure" ones; he preferred the distorted to the straightforward, the ambiguous to the articulated, the inconsistent and equivocal to the direct and clear, "both-and" to "either-or," "black and white and sometimes gray" to "black or white," "richness of meaning" to "clarity of meaning." In *A Significance for A&P Parking Lots, or Learning from Las Vegas* and "Learning from Levittown" he and his collaborators, Denise Scott Brown and Steven Izenour, told where the necessary "messy vitality" might be found. Its cues would come from the "vernacular" architecture of America in the second half of the twentieth century. "Main Street is almost all right," according to one of his dicta. So were the housing developments (Levittown) and the commercial strips (Las Vegas).

Venturi seemed to be saying it was time to remove architecture from the elite world of the universities—from the compounds—and make it once more familiar, comfortable, cozy, and appealing to ordinary people; and to remove it from the level of theory and restore it to the compromising and inconsistent but nevertheless rich terrain of real life.

It was for this reason that people were so baffled by Venturi's buildings themselves. There were very few Venturi buildings, as one might well understand, since he was young and a rebel. (One was for Mother.) At the time *Complexity and Contradiction in Architecture* was published, his only building of any size was the Guild House, a Quaker apartment project for old people in Philadelphia. For such an outspoken young man

Bruno Taut's Hufeisen Siedlung, Berlin, 1926 (top) and Robert Venturi's Guild House, Philadelphia, 1963. It took us thirty-seven years to get this far.

(among architects, anybody under fifty was young), Venturi worked in a somewhat . . . *tentative* way. If he was departing from modernism, he was backing off gingerly, with tiny steps and soft footfalls. In fact, the Guild House bore a curiously strong resemblance to

Bruno Taut's *Red Front!* worker-housing project in Berlin thirty-seven years before. And Bruno, despite the occasional lapse in taste, such as using a color, had devoted his life to *getting it right* in the orthodox manner. At first glance, Venturi's words seemed rebellious. But his designs never seemed anything other than timid.

One clue to the puzzle was the fact that *Complexity and Contradiction* was published in a Museum of Modern Art series. Over at Utopia, Ltd., they did not publish books on "the theoretical background of modern architecture" by apostates.

Venturi's academic credentials were excellent. He had studied architecture at Princeton and was on the faculty at Yale. Like his friend Louis Kahn, he had also studied for a year in Rome as a fellow of the American Academy. In fact, Venturi was the classic architect-intellectual for the new age; young, slender, soft-spoken, cool, ironic, urbane, highly educated, charming with just the right amount of reticence, sophisticated in the lore and the strategies of modern architecture, able to mix plain words with scholarly ones, historical references of the more esoteric sort— to Lutyens, Soane, Vanbrugh, Borromini—with references of the more banal sort—to billboards, electric signs, shopping centers, front-yard mailboxes. *Complexity and Contradiction* appeared with moving and even slightly purple endorsements in the form of an introduction by Yale's prominent architectural historian, Vincent Scully, and a foreword by Arthur Drexler, curator for architecture at the Museum of Modern Art. Scully said that Venturi's work "seems to approach tragic status in the tradition of [Frank] Furness, Louis Sullivan, Wright, and Kahn." (The tragic link between these four, as nearly as one can make out from Scully's text, is that at one time or another they all had to work in Philadelphia).

Studied closely, Venturi's treatise turns out to be not apostasy at all but rather an agile and brilliant skip along the top of the wall of the compound. For a start, he calls it a "gentle" manifesto. But manifestos are not gentle. They are commandments, brought down from the mountaintop, to the boom of thunder. In fact, *Complexity and Contradiction* is no manifesto at all; Venturi is not trying to remove the divinity of art and the authority of taste from the official precinct. He sends out that signal at the very outset:

"I like complexity and contradiction in architecture. I do not like the incoherence or arbitrariness of incompetent architecture nor the precious intricacies of picturesqueness or expressionism." Translation: I, like you, am against the *bourgeois* (picturesque, precious, intricate, arbitrary, incoherent, and incompetent). Moreover, I, like you, have no interest in the merely eccentric (expressionism, in the Saarinen or Mendelsohn manner). Venturi continues: "Instead, I speak of a complex and contradictory architecture based on the richness and ambiguity of modern experience, including that experience which is inherent in art." This turns out to be the most important sentence in the book. *Including that experience which is inherent in art*. Translation: I, like you, am working here within these walls. I am still a member of the compound. Don't worry, the complexities and contradictions I am going to show you, with their "messy vitality," are not going to be drawn from the stupidities of the world outside (except, occasionally, for playful effects) but from our own experience as progeny of the Silver Prince, from *that experience which is inherent in art;* namely, the esoteric lessons of Mies, Corbu, and

Gropius concerning Modern architecture itself. I am going to show you how to make architecture that will amuse, delight, enthrall other architects.

This, then, was the genius of Venturi. He brought modernism into its Scholastic age. Scholasticism in the Dark Ages was theology to test the subtlety of other theologians. Scholasticism in the twentieth century was architecture to test the subtlety of other architects. Venturi became the Roscellinus of modern architecture. Roscellinus, one of the most brilliant of the Scholastics, walked the very edge of heresy and excommunication by suggesting that sheer logic might require that since Jesus Christ, God, and the Holy Ghost were the Three-in-One (the doctrine of the Trinity), then God and the Holy Ghost were also corporeal and had ears, toes, the lot. But he was not excommunicated, and he was not a heretic. He was only pressing logic to its limits and making it do a few one-and-a-half gainers and, one might surmise, trying to make a name for himself. Not for a moment did he question the divinity of God or the existence of the Trinity. And here we have Venturi and, for that matter, Post-Modern architecture, as it is now known, in general.

Not for a moment did Venturi dispute the underlying assumptions of modern architecture: namely, that it was to be for *the people;* that it should be *nonbourgeois* and have *no applied decoration;* that there was a *historical inevitability* to the forms that should be used; and that the architect, from his vantage point inside the compound, would decide what was best for the people and what they inevitably should have.

With considerable wit Venturi redefined those two mythological items on the compound agenda—*the people* and *nonbourgeois*—and then presented the elements of orthodox modern design in prank form, with "Kick me" signs stuck on the back. These became known among architects as "witty" or "ironic references."

In the Venturi cosmology, *the people* could no longer be thought of in terms of the industrial proletariat, the workers with raised fists, engorged brachial arteries, and necks wider than their heads, Marxism's downtrodden masses in the urban slums. *The people* were now the "middle-middle class," as Venturi called them. They lived in suburban developments like Levittown, shopped at the A & P over in the shopping center, and went to Las Vegas on their vacations the way they used to go to Coney Island. The middle-middle folk were not the bourgeoisie. They were the "sprawling" masses, as opposed to the huddled ones. To act snobbishly toward them was to be elitist. And what could be more elitist in this new age, Venturi wanted to know, than the Mies tradition of the International Style, with its emphasis on "heroic and original" forms? Mies' modernism had itself . . . *gone bourgeois!* Modern architects had become obsessed with pure form. He compared the Mies box to a roadside stand in Long Island built in the shape of a duck. The entire building was devoted to expressing a single thought: "Ducks in here." Likewise, the Mies box. It was nothing more than a single expression: "Modern architecture in here." Which made it *expressionism*, right? Heroic, original, elitist, expressionist—how very bourgeois!

So Venturi did to the Mieslings precisely what they had done to Otto Wagner, Josef Hoffmann, and the architects of the Vienna Secession half a century earlier. He consigned them to the garbage barge of bourgeois deviationism.

As for the people, the middle-middle class, Venturi regarded them in precisely the same way that the Silver Prince had regarded the proles of fifty years before. They were intellectually undeveloped, although Venturi was never so gauche as to use such terms. One did not waste time asking them what they liked. As was customary within the compounds, the architect made the decisions in this area.

Venturi's decisions resembled those of Gropius, who had decided that the workers should have low ceilings, small rooms, and narrow hallways. Venturi explained that people are perfectly entitled to have in their buildings the sort of familiar and explicit symbols that applied decoration can provide. So on top of his Guild House he put an enormous television aerial made of gold-anodized aluminum. It was not connected to any television set, however. It was "a symbol for the elderly."

A symbol for the elderly? Scully provided a fuller explanation. Venturi's TV aerial was surprisingly direct, refreshingly candid. "After all, a television aerial at appropriate scale crowns [the building], exactly as it fills—here neither good nor bad but a fact—our old people's lives. Whatever dignity may be in that, Venturi embodies, but he does not lie to us once concerning what the facts are." The phrase "whatever dignity" referred, presumably, to the dignity of aged middle-middle gorks sitting out the golden years narcotized by the tubercular blue gleam of the TV set. Just how much delight, if any, the residents of Guild House found in this familiar and explicit symbol, he did not report.

But so what! The Guild House TV aerial was above all an example of Venturi's gift for the modernist prank. The aerial was a piece of applied ornament and, moreover, a crown, a finial, every bit as much as the "fantastic mooring mast" atop the Empire State Building—i.e., an obvious violation of the International Style. But in fact it was only a TV aerial, which is an ordinary machine-made (good) object whose function requires (good) that it be on top of a building. So only those whom the architect nudged in the ribs would be likely to perceive it as an ornament in the first place. Here we have what became known in the Venturi era as "an ironic reference." Likewise, the aerial's gold finish. Gold, as in Stone's gold leaf, was the epitome of the hopelessly bourgeois in architecture. But *gold-anodized aluminum* was something else again, wasn't it? It was a material conventionally used for the middle-middle people's everyday mass-produced glitter, such as the adjustable strips on the bars of a rolling TV stand.

Venturi implied that if the Guild House had not been run by the Quakers, who are against such graven images, he would have crowned the building with "an open-armed, polychromatic, plaster madonna." He would have . . . but he didn't. Venturi's rebellious exaltations of "the vernacular" led people to look for plaster madonnas and more in his buildings. But somehow they never showed up. Venturi's strategy was to violate the taboo—without violating it. He used red brick (bourgeois) on the upper part of the façade of the Guild House—but it turned out to be a dark red brick especially chosen to match the "smog-smudged" brick of the run-down working-class housing around it (non-bourgeois). He placed a huge column (bourgeois) at the entrance—but it turned out to be undecorated (nonbourgeois), with no capital (nonbourgeois) and no pediment (nonbourgeois). He placed it not to the side but right in the middle of the entryway, making it seem not grander (bourgeois) but more cramped (non-bourgeois). The balconies were given decorative grilles (E. D. Stone bourgeois), but they appeared to have been stamped out in the cheapest possible mass-production process, as if by a punch press (stone-cold nonbourgeois).

O complexity! O contradiction! To violate the taboo—without violating it! Such virtuosity! Venturi had his detractors, but no one in the compounds could help but be impressed. Here was a man skipping, screaming, turning cartwheels on the very edge of the monastery wall—without once slipping or falling.

Of course, a man from Mars—or, we may safely assume, an old person from Philadelphia installed in the Guild House for the remainder of his network dotage—looked at the same building and saw only another typical, drab (smog-smudged red), faceless modern institutional structure. Even within the compounds, there were those who made the mistake of describing Venturi's work in such terms. Philip Johnson and Gordon Bunshaft called Venturi's work "ugly" and "ordinary." They both lived to regret that. Venturi was brilliant in such situations. He was a master of jujitsu. Like the Fauvists and the Cubists of days gone by, he took up every epithet as a glorious motto. "Ugly and ordinary!" he said. Then he turned it into "U & O" and played with that awhile. Better "U & O" than "H & O"—Heroic and Original, which was the stance of Mieslings such as Johnson and Bunshaft. H & O, J & B . . . how very bourgeois.

Venturi often praised the Pop artists of the 1960s, as if they were reestablishing some sort of tie between high art and popular culture. Venturi's strategy was, in fact, precisely like that of the Pop artists—and neither had any interest, beyond the playful and camp, in

popular culture. Pop Art was not a rebellion. The Pop
artists, no less than the abstract expressionists whom
they eclipsed, still religiously observed the central
tenets of modernism concerning flatness ("the integrity
of the picture plane") and nonillusionism. They were
careful to do only pictures of other pictures—labels,
comic-strip panels, flags, pages of numbers—so that
their fellow hierophants in the Modern movement
would realize that they were not actually returning to
realism. Jasper Johns' proponents said that his pictures of flags and numbers, for example, were the *flat-
test* and most *nonillusionistic* paintings yet, because
they were of things that were by their very nature two-
dimensional and abstract. Pop was a leg-pull, a mis-
chievous but, at bottom, respectful wink at the
orthodoxy of the day.

For many younger architects, Venturi's Big Wink
was irresistible. The man was a genius. He had figured
out the perfect strategy for routing the old crowd, the
Mies-box people, without trying to dismantle the compound system itself. Venturi had found their vulner-
able spots: first, their dreadful solemnity and high
seriousness; and second, their age and remoteness
from modern life. Their ideas of machine forms and
mass production came from the period before the First
World War. Their Mieslings' approach to the goal of
being nonbourgeois had been to take the "industrial
vernacular" from "the other side of the tracks," as
Venturi put it, and introduce it to "the civic areas of
the city." Venturi was doing the same thing, but he
was updating the process. He was using "the commercial vernacular" (the Las Vegas strip) and "the merchant builders' vernacular" (the suburban housing
development). Down with wide-flange beams. Up with
a TV aerial here and a polka-dot punch-press balus-

trade there. That was the beauty of it. Venturi was
upholding a central tenet of the compounds, after all.
He was sticking to the wrong side of the tracks. He
was keeping the nonbourgeois faith.

There were those who, like Venturi himself, thought
the source of arcane "reference" (the terminology of
Structural linguistics was now taken up like a monocle) should be the middle-middle sprawling masses
outside the walls. Charles Moore, formerly dean of
architecture at Yale and now at UCLA, became the
master of the camp historical reference. Moore would
place a big piece of Victorian hyper-ogeed molding
(bourgeois and a half) over a doorway in a private
home—but with the following touches that snatched it
from the jaws of apostasy at the last moment: 1. He
put the molding only at the top, leaving the rest of the
doorway with the usual mean plaster worker-housing
frame. 2. He used not casing or architrave molding,
which one usually sees around a door frame (if one has
to look at such retrograde sights at all), but picture
molding, from which picture frames are supposed to
be hung, by wire or decorative ribbon. 3. In case there
was someone who still didn't get it, he attached a little
strip of mirror vertically at one end of the molding, so
that it was repeated for emphasis. But for emphasis on
what? Why, on the fact that this was only "an ironic
historical reference." Intellectually, the molding remained as detached and remote as if it were behind a
glass case in a museum of folk art.

Gradually, a Venturi, or "Pop Architecture," movement began to form. It included Moore, Hugh Hardy,
Moore's friend William Turnbull, and Robert Stern.
As editor of the magazine *Perspecta* when he was an
architecture student at Yale, Stern had run part of

Complexity and Contradiction a year before the book was published, and had helped call Venturi to the attention of Vincent Scully. By now, Scully served the Venturi wing of American architecture the way Guillaume Apollinaire had served the Cubists, which is to say, as scholar, counsel, and special pleader.

Beyond any doubt, Scully had established his credentials as a prophet. In his introduction to *Complexity and Contradiction in Architecture* he had described it as the most important piece of writing on architecture since Le Corbusier's *Vers une architecture*. The next few years had proved him right. Venturi was the first architect to create an impórtant change inside the compound of the Silver Prince. Like Roscellinus, Venturi had his enemies, and some of them were bitter. But one and all were caught up in the utterly serious game he had originated: architecture of infinite subtlety for the delectation and astonishment of other architects. The new arcana revealed!—one monk to the other.

The recession of the early 1970s intensified the process. The recession wrecked the business structure of American architecture almost as thoroughly as had the Great Depression forty years before. There had been a tremendous building boom during the 1960s; practically every major downtown in the Eastern United States had been rebuilt in a short time. Many new architecture firms had been founded, and many older firms had swollen to more than a hundred employees. The expansion had come to a natural end at the same time as the financial slide had begun. Overnight, it seemed, thirty to forty percent of all architects were out of work. Firms with two hundred employees were suddenly reduced to ten. Senior partners were answering the telephones. Draftsmen were promoted to

The Whites. Architecture's about-face avant-garde, marching resolutely back to the 1920s and Corbu's early phase, with R & R at Gerrit Rietveld's. Top: Peter Eisenman, House II. Middle: Richard Meier, Douglas House. Bottom: Charles Gwathmey, Bridgehampton residence.

vice presidents. That way, instead of receiving salaries, they could share in profits, which no longer existed. Then came the exodus. Half of America's architects seemed to be working, if they were working at all, for the Shah of Iran. Forty percent seemed to be working for King Saud the Good. The rest stayed behind to vie for fame within the intellectual competition of the academies.

In 1972, a new compound, known as the Whites, or the New York Five, made its bid with a book entitled *Five Architects,* the five being Peter Eisenman, Michael Graves, John Hejduk, Richard Meier, and Charles Gwathmey. They played Anselm or Abelard to Venturi's Roscellinus. In their bid to appear original without violating the fundamental assumptions of modernism, they took the position that the true way would be found not in the land of the sprawling middle-middles but in a return to first principles. Their idea was to return to the purest of all the purists, Dr. Purism himself, Le Corbusier, and explore the paths he had indicated. Their Apollinaire was Colin Rowe, a professor of architecture at Cornell who had written an influential exegesis of Le Corbusier's work. They were called the Whites because practically all their buildings were white, inside and out, like the maestro's.

Their position was that Corbu had opened up a universe of forms that were right and inevitable because they came from the very core—"the deep structure," to use Eisenman's term—of the meaning of architecture itself. The *meaning* of architecture? For most who approached the Whites cold, this was a baffling notion. But . . . ah!—the Whites were ready for all the puzzled looks.

By now the philosophy—and the jargon—of French Structural linguistics was highly fashionable in American universities. Even Venturi, with all his talk about "vernaculars," "codes," "references," and "ambiguities," had been affected by it. Structuralism had originated in France in what might be called a Late or Mannerist Marxist mist. The Structuralists assumed that language (and therefore meaning) has an immutable underlying structure, growing out of the very nature of the central nervous system. Instinctively, the ruling classes, the capitalists, the bourgeoisie, have appropriated this structure for their own purposes and saturated it with a bewildering internal propaganda.

If this notion in itself seemed a bit incomprehensible, that didn't matter. What mattered was that Structuralists were people dedicated to stripping the whole bourgeois mess down to clean bare bones. Structuralists were beneficial to the people by the very nature of their work. So there was no need to get messily political about it. The same misty goodness enveloped the Whites. The simple truth was that they could scarcely have cared less about politics. In any case, they didn't have to. It was taken for granted that Structuralist experiments were good for the people.

The work of the Whites you could tell at a glance. Their buildings were white . . . and baffling. They could barely stand to introduce the occasional black or gray touch, such as the band of black painted at the base of a wall to do the work of the old (bourgeois) baseboards. They were convinced that the way to be nonbourgeois, in the new age, was to be scrupulously pure, as Corbu had been scrupulously pure, and to be baffling. Baffling was *their* contribution.

Corbu was a pane of glass compared to, say, Peter Eisenman, an architect who ran the Institute for Architecture and Urban Studies in New York, which put out the two major organs of the Whites, *Oppositions* and *Skyline*. Eisenman was Corbu, if Corbu had ever gone to Holland and been hypnotized by Gerrit Rietveld. Eisenman designed white buildings that were Expressed Structure Heaven. They were like a piece of serial music by Milton Babbitt. The outsider found them utterly incomprehensible. The insider—the fellow compound architect—could detect that there was some sort of pattern, some sort of complex paradigm, underlying all the strange angles and projections, but he couldn't figure out what on earth it was. One's own esoteric soul cried out for an explanation.

But Eisenman's explanations were not much help, even to the initiate. Eisenman had gone all the way with the linguistics business . . . Others were talking about *syntactical nuances* and the *semiology of the infrastructure* and the *semantics of the superstructure* and the *morphemes of negative space* and the *polyphemes of architectonic afterimage*. They would talk about such things as "the articulation of the perimeter of the perceived structure and its dialogue with the surrounding landscape." (This caused a Harvard logician to ask, "What did the landscape have to say?" The architect had nothing verbatim to report.) But they were all United Press International rewrite men, simple to a fault, compared with Eisenman. Eisenman's great genius was to use relatively clear words from the linguistic lingo and lead one's poor brain straight into the Halusian Gulp.

"Syntactic meaning as defined here," he would say, "is not concerned with the meaning that accrues to elements or actual relationships between elements but rather with the *relationship* between *relationships*."

Eisenman was beautiful. He could lead any man alive into the Gulp in a single sentence. Eisenman was such a purist that in the few instances when houses he designed were built, he did not refer to them by the names of the owners, as other architects did (e.g., Wright's Robie House, Rietveld's Schroeder House). He referred to them by numbers: House I, House II, and so on. It was as if they didn't belong to anybody, no matter who had paid for them. They belonged to the deep structure of architecture; and, if one need edit, to history. His confrere Hejduk referred to his houses by numbers for a different reason. None of them had ever been built. They were all Corbu theoretical treatises in two dimensions, such as his "One-Half House," which consisted of floor plans and axonometric schemes based on half a circle, half a diamond, and half a square. The one piece of constructed work Hejduk had to his credit was the renovation of the interior of the main building of Cooper Union in New York, where he was dean of the school of architecture. It was remarkable enough: a Corbu boat inserted, against all odds, inside a Beaux-Arts bottle. I saw it for the first time when I attended the Cooper Union commencement exercises in 1980. I could barely concentrate on the event at hand. Cooper Union had been designated a landmark building, so that Hejduk had not been able to touch the exterior. The exterior looked pretty much as it must have when Fred A. Petersen designed it a hundred and twenty-five years before. It was a great brownstone waltz of arch windows, caesurae, cornices, and loggias, in the Italian palazzo style, taking up an entire block. And inside? Inside the old masonry shell, at enormous expense, Hejduk had blown up Corbu's little Villa Savoye like a balloon. The white walls, the ramps, the pipe railings, the cylinders . . . It was all quite bizarre. And why had he done it? Because, being a true compound architect, a true White, a true Neo-Purist, *he could do nothing else*. Petersen had designed huge windows along the stairways. The idea was to illuminate them as much as possible by sunlight. But this meant that anyone walking down the stairs could look out and see big chunks of Petersen's damnable brown bourgeois masonry. So Hejduk meticulously enclosed the stairs in white Corbu cylinders, converting them into stairwells. Overhead, in the gloom, at each landing, there was a single unadorned 22-watt fluorescent circlet bulb of the sort known in New York as the Landlord's Halo.

7
Silver-White, Silver-Gray

IN 1973 THE VENTURI, or Pop, architects took on the Whites in an attack that, in the planning stage, seemed like a great lark. This was a piece called "Five on Five," published in *Architectural Forum*. The idea was that five architects from the Venturi wing— Moore, Stern, Jaquelin Robertson, Allan Greenberg, and Romaldo Giurgola—would review *Five Architects*. Stern led off with a piece entitled "Stompin' at the Savoye." Most of Stern's teammates opened their rounds with a few bows and feints of professional courtesy, but Stern got into the spirit of the fight right off. He described Colin Rowe as the Five's "intellectual guru," a man stuck in the "hothouse aesthetics of the 1920s," faithful to "the most questionable aspects of Le Corbusier's philosophy"—and resentful of Vincent Scully's accurate claim that Venturi existed on a plane with Le Corbusier as a "form-giver." He said Hejduk was doing the only thing his designs were good for: "paper architecture." As for Eisenman, his theorizing gave Stern "a headache," and his houses were a "superfluity of walls, beams and columns" that added up not to "deep structure" but to claustrophobia. He called Graves and Meier "compulsively modern" and found Meier capable of doing "lumpish" work besides. Robertson tried to be generous and balanced in dealing with the work of Meier and Gwathmey, but when he got to Graves, he couldn't hold back anymore. In Graves, he said, one came upon all that was "weak" and "wrongheaded" in Neo-Corbu. His houses were "crawling inside and out with a sort of nasty modern ivy in the way of railings, metal trellises, unexplained pipes, exposed beams, inexplicable and obtuse tubes—most to no apparent real or architectural purpose."

The Whites screamed in protest. They screamed so bitterly that never again have American architects attacked one another head-on in print. They screamed, but in fact the Venturi Five had done them a great favor. They had made the Whites seem like one of two great armies battling on the plains of heaven for the soul of the modern movement. The very future of American architecture seemed to hang in the balance of the combat between the Whites and the Pop architects, or Venturians or Yale–Philadelphia Axis . . . or whatever they should be called. Somebody came up with "the Grays," which was simpler. So it became the Whites versus the Grays. That was all you heard in the universities, the Whites *vs.* the Grays; the young architects began to choose up sides. The fact that both sides remained obedient to the tenets of modernism tended to be lost in the excitement.

The younger European architects couldn't believe what was happening. Those eternal colonials, those

most obedient natives, the Americans, had stolen the
lead in, of all things, architectural theory. They were
having a great time for themselves, even in the midst
of the commercial slump in the profession. The same
slump had hit European architecture. In some re-
spects, it had been even worse. Private commissions
scarcely existed any longer. Architects sat about
nibbling at government feasibility studies, anything.
Why not do what the Americans were doing? A
theoretical architect could make a reputation without
commissions. At the very least, he might obtain lec-
tureships, and his drawings might be worth money.

For whatever reason, the Rationalists were born at
this moment. The leading Rationalists were an Italian,
Aldo Rossi, a Spaniard, Ricardo Bofill, and two
brothers from Luxembourg, Leon and Robert Krier.
The Rationalists were like the Whites in that they be-
lieved that the true and inevitable way of modernism
was to go back to first principles. But they felt the
Whites had not gone back far enough. The Rationalists
liked to go back to the eighteenth century at least; and
the early Renaissance was best of all. The Rationalists
wanted to do pre-nineteenth-century buildings—
stripped of all bourgeois ornament. The idea was that
they were going back before the industrial revolution,
back before capitalism; which is to say, back before
capitalism could pollute architecture with its corrup-
tion.

The Marxist mist enveloping Rationalism was even
denser, muggier, and more sentimental than the one
that enveloped the Structuralists. The Rationalists had
the romantic proletcult notion that the master
craftsmen of the Renaissance built from out of the
natural and inevitable impulses of *the people,* as if out
of some sort of structuralism of the motor reflexes.

The fact that these buildings were generally commissioned and paid for by kings, despots, dukes, pontiffs, and other autocrats didn't matter. At least they weren't capitalists.

Soon the Rationalists were adding a certain primitive zest to architectural debate in the United States. At architectural conferences in the United States, they went about yelling "Immoral!" at everyone they disagreed with. They were embarrassing but fascinating. Venturi made them furious. "Immoral!" Venturi extolled the very gutter of capitalism in its modern phase, namely, the commercial strip. "Immoral! Corrupt! American!"

As for their own work, it looked . . . well, oddly Fascist. In both Italy and Germany, Fascist architecture had featured Classical designs with the applied

Apartments in Milan, 1970, by the pride of the Rats, Aldo Rossi. Bourgeois-proofed architecture for the European school of holy-rolling, foot-washing, primitive Marxists.

ornament removed or conventionalized. When Rationalists like Leon Krier were reminded of this, they became unglued. Fascist or not, Aldo Rossi's work was eerie. With the architraves, lintels, compound arches, and the like removed, his Renaissance windows ended up as rather lugubrious shaded voids. Soon the Rationalists were known as the Rats.

British architects tended to be skeptical of the theorizing, but they were intrigued all the same. A young American architect, Charles Jencks, something of a Venturi–Moore man in his own work, went to England and published a book called *The Language of Post-Modern Architecture,* which catalogued and analyzed all the new currents. Whatever his status as an architect, he immediately established himself as the wittiest and most knowledgeable architectural writer in the business. The term Post-Modernism caught on as the name for all developments since the general exhaustion of modernism itself. As Jencks himself remarked with some felicity, Post-Modernism was perhaps too comforting a term. It told you what you were leaving without committing you to any particular destination. He was right. The new term itself tended to create the impression that modernism was over because it had been superseded by something new. In fact, the Post-Modernists, whether Whites, Grays, or Rats, had never emerged from the spare little box fashioned in the 1920s by Gropius, Corbu, and the Dutchmen. For the most part, they were busy doing nothing more than working changes on the same tight little concepts, now sixty years old, for the benefit of one another.

In May of 1980 one of the Whites, Michael Graves, professor of architecture at Princeton, was the lone architect amid thirty-seven artists, composers, and

writers receiving awards from the American Academy
and Institute of Arts and Letters at their annual cere-
monies at the Academy's grand auditorium in New
York. Graves stepped forward from his seat onstage
and received the Arnold W. Brunner Memorial Prize
for Architecture. Seventeen awards later, Gordon
Bunshaft, now seventy-one and an elder of the Institute, was called on to read the citations for five painters and hand out envelopes with checks inside. After
disbursing the last of them, Bunshaft turned toward
the audience and said:

"I suppose this is something you don't see every
day, an architect handing out money to artists."

The audience laughed faintly, acknowledging that a
pleasantry had been attempted but not quite getting it.

"But, then, a lot of things have changed," said Bunshaft. "We used to give prizes to architects for doing
buildings. Now we give prizes to architects for drawing pictures."

Then he sat down. Not a peep out of the audience.
Only a few souls—compound architects one and all—
had the faintest notion of what he meant. Bunshaft had
made no mention of Graves, who was seated behind
him on the stage, nor did he look his way. But Graves
was the only architect who had received an award, and
furthermore it was true: he had won the award for
drawings. Or, rather, for his drawings, for his theories,
and for his status as Princeton's resident White, or
Neo-Purist. Not for buildings, in any event. You could
count Graves' built structures on one hand. "Structures"—an addition here, an alteration there, and a
few small houses. They all looked like Gerrit Rietveld
on a terrific bender, thanks to the inexplicable "modern ivy" of railings, tubes, and beams Robertson had
complained about.

But so what! In the new mental atmosphere, in mod-

The sort of Corbusier-style drawing for which Graves is famous: a proposed Cultural Center Bridge across the Red River, between Fargo, North Dakota, and Moorhead, Minnesota.

ern architecture's Scholastic phase, Graves' career shone with an unmistakable radiance. There was something sordid about doing a lot of building. Even among the Whites, the New York Five, Gwathmey and Meier were spoken of, *sotto voce,* as the lightweights, chiefly because they had going practices and actually made money from architecture. Meier ranked above Gwathmey because, in addition to building buildings, he taught at Harvard and enunciated suitably obscure theories. They were not so profoundly obscure as Graves', however. When Graves talked about "the multiple readings inherent in a code of abstraction" and "a level of participation that involves

Michael Graves' Benacerraf House addition. Underneath all the metal Gerrit Rietveld ivy are a breakfast room and playroom.

the reciprocal act of ourselves with the figure of the building," he almost achieved the Structuralist heights of Eisenman. (Almost, but not quite; Eisenman had managed to become *perfectly* obscure.) The Graves approach was known and talked about in the architecture department of every important university in the country. His watercolor renderings of his own unbuilt buildings were mauve, blue, swift, and terribly beautiful, like a storm. *Corbu!* One had only to say "Michael," as his friends called him, and every aspiring architect on the circuit knew it was Michael Graves.

You couldn't say the same about Gordon Bunshaft—despite the scores of behemoth glass buildings he had designed or inspired. Within the university compounds you could say "Gordon" or even "Gordon Bunshaft," and all you would get would be a look as heavily glazed as Lever House.

The hell with the behemoth buildings! Every heads-up architect knew you had to excel, first of all, in the intellectual competition of the compounds. The ideal career was the Corbu career. There had been an unmistakable *purity* about Corbu, in his career as in his designs. Corbu had triumphed through intellect and genius alone, through manifestos, treatises, speeches, debates, drawings, visionary plans, and the sheer moral force of his mission. He had become one of the greatest architects of the world, respected and admired by every avant-garde architect; had created that Radiant City which was himself, Corbu—without benefit of commissions, clients, budgets, buildings. All those things had come his way later. Eventually he would be handed commissions such as the Chandigarh complex in the Indian province of the Punjab. The clients, the governments, the builders, the peoples of the world, had come to him because he *was* the Radiant City, which had been a creation of his mind and his mind alone. They had fought, at last, to set foot inside his compound, which had been called, appropriately enough, "Purism."

This same process was only beginning for Graves. Portland, Oregon, had just commissioned him to do its new Public Services Building. There was a furor in Portland over both the proposed design and the manner of Graves' selection—much was made of the influence of Philip Johnson—but the fact remained that it was Graves' intellectual victories within the university compounds that had led to this, his first large building, or at least the first one that was likely to be built. There were also incidental but lucrative dividends. Furniture manufacturers began to seek out the Post-Modernist stars to design showrooms. Graves was commissioned to do showrooms for the Sunar Company in New York, Chicago, Los Angeles, and Houston. Venturi was commissioned to do a new showroom in New York for the best known of the firms specializing in modern furniture, Knoll International.

By the late 1970s, the more finely attuned young architects were devising a new approach to the business of architecture. They were creating firms that combined the two tracks of modern architectural competition—building buildings and theorizing about architecture—in a single entity. Which is to say, they turned their companies into compounds. They offered a particular approach to design, a set of forms, a philosophy—and a philosopher, a spokesman, who was scholarly, profound, even abstruse, should protocol require it. Arquitectonica, SITE, and Friday Architects were among the most prominent. Life in the company compound even had a touch of the communal existence of the Bauhaus or de Stijl. SITE's James Wines became much in demand at architectural conferences in the United States and Europe. His Magritte-style storefronts for the Best discount-store chain were as much sculpture or "environmental art," to use one of the new terms of the day, as architecture. In any case, SITE's expenditure of so much talent and intellect on a chain of stores infuriated the Rats. They thought and thought and finally came up with a word or two for Wines and SITE: "Immoral! Corrupt! American!"

For the ambitious architect, having a theory became as vital and natural as having a telephone. Finally, the pressure even got to John Portman. He decided it was time he elaborated a philosophy. He wrote an essay for *Architectural Record*. Well, Portman may have changed the look of the American downtown, but in this league he was a novice. His message was entirely too clear and comprehensible. About as deep and dumfounding as a raindrop, it was. People like trees and water and human scale in public buildings, and they should have them . . . theories at the what-people-want level. Well, as one can imagine—how they sniggered at poor John Portman over that!

Nevertheless, it seemed vital, even to the commercial giants, to get in on the new game, at the very least. Last December, Gordon Bunshaft's firm, Skidmore, Owings & Merrill, the commercial giants of the old Miesling glass-box vogue, took a rather desperate step. They invited the editors of the *Harvard Architecture Review* to put together a private panel of architects who would discuss new developments in Post-Modernism with them. The *Review* came up with Graves, Stern, Steven Peterson, and Jorge Silvetti. They sat at a U-shaped table at the Harvard Club in New York and confronted a team of Skidmore, Owings & Merrill architects—and lectured them as if they were architecture students receiving their first studio critiques. The Skidmore group showed slides of their new work, by way of proving that their work was by no means restricted to glass boxes of the Lever House tower sort. The fact was that they were also doing squat glass boxes with curved corners and the like. The Post-Mods, whether White or Gray, were having none of that. Stern said: "The kinds of buildings Skidmore builds are boring—tall or short, fat or thin, if you've seen one you've seen them all." The Skidmores didn't even bother to fight back.

O Destiny . . . At no time did it seem to strike anyone present as funny that here were the leading architects—commercially—in the field of large public building in America, and they were willingly—willingly?—they *begged* for it—sitting still for a dressing-down by four architects who, between them, could claim few buildings larger than a private house. Well, what was funny about that? Such was the hold of the compound mentality, of the new Scholasticism, on the architectural profession.

In 1976 Vincent Scully refused an American Institute of Architects award for architectural history on the grounds that they had refused to induct Robert Venturi into their College of Fellows. It was no honor, said Scully, to receive an award from an organization that was so insensitive—since Venturi was "the most important architect of my generation."

As to whether this assertion had any aesthetic merit—well, *de gustibus non est disputandum.* But in terms of Venturi's influence on other architects, Scully once again had a point. Venturi's wing, the Grays, was slowly winning the great battle on the plains of heaven. The Whites were beginning to abandon their Purist position—and their Structuralist jargon. (In the universities, Structuralism itself was being challenged by the new notion of Entropy, which held that there were no neat, logical *deep structures* after all; it was an uncertain, stochastic, Barnum & Bailey world.) Graves began to work extremely subtle variations on the Venturi approach. He sought a higher synthesis of White and Gray, one worthy of Abelard or Duns Scotus. He was still using White "codes of abstraction"—but the codes referred to the familiar architectural environment of Venturi's poor middle-middles. For example, in an addition to a house in Princeton he created a post-and-beam projection that looked like a David Smith sculpture as adapted by Rietveld—and painted it blue. This was supposed to *resonate* with the familiar middle-middle blue sky overhead as one walked under it. Whether anybody actually got that or not was not nearly so important as recognizing the sophistication of the approach. Later, Graves edged toward Moore's position of playing Classical forms, notably columns, against modern façades so thin that, quite deliberately, they had the look of cardboard. The results resembled the backdrops in the typical resort community production of *Aïda*.

The continual playing with Classical elements, by Moore, Graves, Venturi, and many others, tended to create the impression that some sort of revival of the Classical tradition was taking place. Naturally, this was not so, for that would have been apostasy. The architects themselves always bridled at the suggestion. For example, Jorge Silvetti and his partner Rodolfo Machado said of their proposed Steps of Providence (for Providence, Rhode Island): "No one single classical element in a 'pure' state can be found. They are all transformations of classical motives, transformed to the point of being either aclassical or anticlassical." Likewise, in 1978 Venturi announced his new definition of architecture as "shelter with decoration on it" and said that he knew this would be "shocking." By now everyone could only yawn, because, of course, Venturi's visual translation of his own definition would not be shocking. As an example he presented drawings for *A Country House Based on Mount Vernon*. "The detailing is simplified, flattened, and generalized," he said. "Reproducing it [Washington's Mount Vernon] as a house is somewhat like Jasper Johns making a painting out of the American flag." So much for shelter with decoration on it. Bob Venturi was only camping it up a bit more, making more of his brilliant and amusing ironic references. At the heart of real architectural decoration, as the eclectic architects of the nineteenth century understood, was an impulse toward enrichment and embellishment, not flattening and generalization. By 1978 it had become apparent that not even with a gun at his temple could Venturi have produced an original and embellished piece of decoration. He simply could not make his hand move over a piece of paper in that manner. He could not manage such a motor response. He remained, after all this, the most loyal of subjects of the Silver Prince.

For any architect to have explored an avenue such as a new, straightforward (non-ironic), exuberant (non-camp) system of decoration for American architecture in the late twentieth century would have been a revolutionary development. It would also have been heretical. No ambitious American architect, if he had his head on straight, was going to try it. And no architect who tried it was likely to have any significant effect on the course of American architecture. The entire structure of the compounds and the clerisy, with all their rewards, psychic and mundane, would have to be dismantled first.

By 1978, the evidence that Venturi was winning the battle of the compounds was decisive. Philip Johnson released renderings and models of his new corporate headquarters for AT&T, to be constructed on Madison Avenue in New York. It became the most famous unbuilt building of the 1970s. The most devoted Miesling of them all had designed a building with a top that seemed to have been lifted straight off a Chippendale

A model of the soon-to-be-built AT&T headquarters in New York. The design is Philip Johnson's, but the victory is Robert Venturi's.

highboy. Philip Johnson! Up off his knees at last! After forty years!

Johnson had learned one lesson well. He had finally realized that in an age of esoteric, intramural competition among artists, it was folly to try to counter a new style by meeting it head on and calling it "ugly" or "ordinary." (So did the bourgeois.) The trick was to *leapfrog* the new style and say: "Yes, but look! I have established a more avant-garde position . . . way out here."

Venturi's partisans were furious. They claimed that Johnson had stolen the idea of the highboy crown and its broken pediment straight from Venturi, from a piece he wrote in the March 1968 *Architectural Forum*. Venturi had mentioned a motel near Jefferson's Monticello in Virginia. "The sign for the Motel Monticello, a silhouette of an enormous Chippendale highboy, is visible on the highway before the motel itself." Well, swell, Bob. But Venturi had never dared go so far as to actually put such a thing on top of a building. It was as if Venturi had actually put his plaster madonna up on top of the Guild House and not merely talked about it and put up the Old Dotage Home TV Aerial instead. Johnson's AT&T highboy verged perilously, perilously, perilously close to . . . *sheer naked unmistakable apostasy!*

And there are signs today that it is being interpreted as such. Inside the compound, one begins to hear Johnson talked of in the way Edward Durell Stone was talked of after the unveiling of the Taj Maria.

But Johnson remained as artful a tactician as Venturi. In speeches and interviews he managed to let the faithful know that in such areas as his attitude toward the client he remained the classic modernist. He told how his client, AT&T, had been "so perspicacious that they gave us a clue. They said, 'Please don't give us a flat top.'"

It was very reassuring! One could see the scene: the CEO, the chairman of the board, and the whole selection committee, representing the biggest corporation in the history of man, approach the architect, making imaginary snowballs with their hands and saying, "Please, Mr. Johnson, we don't mean to interfere in any way. All we ask is, please, sir, don't give us a flat top."

And what did the client think of what he got? Oh, that was a laugh and a half, said Johnson. "The chairman of the board said, 'Now *that's* a building!' In other words, a building is a building; but a building isn't a building if it's a glass box. What's in their minds as to what a building is, I'm not quite sure. It's like saying, *'That* is a house!' when you finally see a salt-box."

Inside the compound, one could relax a bit. Johnson had committed apostasy, probably, but *they* still hadn't *gotten* it. They only paid for it. The outside world remained as out of it as ever. The new masses still struggled in the middle-middle ooze. The bourgeoisie was still baffled. The light of the Silver Prince still shone here in the Radiant City. And the client still took it like a man.